Charles Johnson Maynard

The Naturalist's Guide in Collecting and Preserving Objects of

Natural History

With a complete catalogue of the birds of eastern Massachusetts

Charles Johnson Maynard

The Naturalist's Guide in Collecting and Preserving Objects of Natural History
With a complete catalogue of the birds of eastern Massachusetts

ISBN/EAN: 9783337218300

Printed in Europe, USA, Canada, Australia, Japan

Cover: Foto ©ninafisch / pixelio.de

More available books at **www.hansebooks.com**

BAIRD'S SPARROW.

THE

NATURALIST'S GUIDE

IN COLLECTING AND PRESERVING

OBJECTS OF NATURAL HISTORY,

WITH

A COMPLETE CATALOGUE OF THE BIRDS OF EASTERN MASSACHUSETTS.

By C. J MAYNARD.

WITH ILLUSTRATIONS BY E. L. WEEKS

SALEM:
THE NATURALISTS' AGENCY.
BOSTON: ESTES & LAURIAT.
1877.

INTRODUCTION.

THE great need of a good illustrated work to guide young naturalists in collecting and preserving objects of natural history has induced me to prepare the present Manual. In this attempt I hope I have been in some degree successful. I have spared no pains to bring together, in a comprehensive form, the results of many years of experience in collecting and preserving objects of natural history, both for private cabinets and for scientific museums.

No popular work of this kind has before been published in America. Throughout the present work I have endeavored to encourage the young to engage in the ennobling study of Natural History, and to join the band of young naturalists so rapidly increasing in our land.

I trust the reader will not by any means keep the teachings of this book secret, as some taxidermists are wont to counsel, but spread it broadcast among those who would profit by the information I have herein attempted to convey. It is intended for the NATURALIST, whoever and wherever he may be ; and as it comes from a colaborer in the common field, it will, perhaps, be well received.

All of Part First is original. In preparing objects of natural history I have in a great degree invented methods of my own, and have not given in this work a single one that I have not tested and proved equal to all others, if not superior. To avoid confusion, I have given only the method which experience has taught me to le the best.

In this connection my thanks are due to Mr. E. L. Weeks, whose excellent illustrations will be found to add greatly to the value of the work.

In Part Second I have thought proper to add a catalogue of the birds of Eastern Massachusetts, with notes, as tending to enable the collector to obtain the rarer species more readily, by specifying the localities and peculiar haunts in which they have been found by others. The critical notes may, perhaps, be perused with interest by the more experienced ornithologist.

CONTENTS.

PART I.

CHAPTER I.

COLLECTING AND PRESERVING BIRDS.

CHAPTER II.

COLLECTING AND PRESERVING MAMMALS.

CHAPTER III.

COLLECTING AND PRESERVING INSECTS FOR THE CABINET.

CHAPTER IV.

COLLECTING AND PRESERVING FISHES AND REPTILES.

CHAPTER V.

MISCELLANEOUS COLLECTIONS.

CHAPTER VI.

PART II.

LIST AND EXPLANATION OF PLATES.

FRONTISPIECE. *Centronyx Bairdii,* Baird. — Baird's Sparrow, taken at Ipswich, Mass.

PLATE I.* INSTRUMENTS used in preparing birds, etc., and for blowing eggs. *Fig.* 1, Common Pliers; *Fig.* 2, Cutting Pliers; *Fig.* 3, Tweezers; *Fig.* 4, Scalpel; *Figs.* 5 and 6, Egg-drills; *Fig.* 7, Blow-pipe; *Fig.* 8, Hook for removing embryos from eggs.

PLATE II. — WINGS, showing the positions of the different feathers, as follows: —

Fig. 1. *Wing of a Red tailed Hawk* (*Buteo borealis,* Vieill.). — a indicates the primaries, or quills; b, secondaries; c, tertiaries; d, scapularies; g, greater wing-coverts; f, lesser wing-coverts; e, spurious wing, or quills.

Fig 2. *Wing of a Coot, or Mud Hen* (*Fulica Americana,* Gmelin). — a indicates the primaries, or quills; b, secondaries; c, tertiaries; d, scapularies; e, spurious wing, or quills.

The tertiaries and scapularies are elongated in most of the aquatic birds, and in some of the Waders. They are *always prominent,* if not elongated, on long-winged birds, such as the Eagles, Hawks, Owls, Vultures, etc.; while they are only rudimentary on short-winged birds, such as the Thrushes, Warblers, Sparrows, etc.

PLATE III. HEAD OF THE BALD EAGLE (*Haliætus leucocephalus,* Savigny), showing the different parts, as follows: — a, the throat; b, chin; c, commissure, or the folding edges of the mandibles; d, under mandible; s, gonys; p, gape; g, upper mandible; h, culmen; i, tip; j, base of bill; k, cere (naked skin at the base of the upper mandible, prominent in the rapacious birds); l, frontal feathers; m, lores; n, crown; o, occiput.

* Plates I , IV., V., VI., VIII., IX , X., and the frontispiece will be more fully explained hereafter.

The irides are the colored circles that surround the pupil. The color of these decides the so-called "color of the eye."

PLATE IV. ILLUSTRATES PREPARING SKINS — *Figs.* 1 and 2. Corrugated board, used in drying skins; d, skin on the board, in the proper position. *Fig.* 3. A "skin" prepared for scientific use; ♂, label on which is marked the number and sex.

PLATE V. DISSECTED SONG SPARROW (*Melospiza melodia*, Baird), illustrating the sexes in the breeding season, as follows : — *Fig.* 1. An adult female (♀); 1, 1, peculiar yellow glands; 2, ovary; 3, oviduct; 4, lungs. *Fig.* 2. An adult male (♂); 1, lungs; 2, peculiar yellow glands; 3, 3, testicles.

PLATE VI. DISSECTED SONG SPARROW, illustrating the sexes of the young-of-the-year, in autumn, as follows : — *Fig.* 1. A young male (♂); 1, lungs; 2, 2, yellow glands; 3, 3, testicles. *Fig* 2. A young female (♀); 1, 1, yellow glands; 2, ovary; 3, lungs; 4, oviduct.

PLATE VII. OUTLINE OF GROUSE, showing the position of the different parts, as follows : — a, the back; b, rump; c, upper tail-coverts; d, under tail-coverts; e, vent; f, tibia; g, tarsi; h, breast; i, side; j, neck; k, hind neck; l, abdomen; m, feet; n, throat.

PLATE VIII. ILLUSTRATES MOUNTING BIRDS. — *Figs.* 1, 2. Artificial body; a, bone of leg; b, wire bent; c, wire clenched; f, h, tail wire. *Fig.* 3. Mounted bird; a, perpendicular line, showing the position of the head compared with the feet and base of the stand; b, b, wires for retaining the upper part of the wing in position; c, c. wires for retaining the lower part of the wing in position; e, e, wires for the tail; d, showing the tail-feathers plaited; f, stand. *Fig.* 4 Stand for mounting birds with the wings extended; h, h, parallel wires; c, wires bent; a, block of wood for the bottom of the stand. *Fig.* 5. Head of Cedar-Bird, to illustrate the elevating of the crest; g, cotton on the pin; b, feathers of the crest in position on the cotton.

PLATE IX. ILLUSTRATES MOUNTING MAMMALS — *Fig.* 1. A, plank for supporting iron rods; 8, iron rod for supporting head; 14, cap, nut, and screw for fastening the end of the rod in the skull; 7, 7, 7, 7, iron rods to support the body; 5. 6, 5, 6, caps, etc. for fastening the upper ends of the rods to the plank; 17, 17, 17, 17, caps, etc. for fastening the lower part of the rods to the stand (10); 15, wire for supporting the tail; 16, 16, 16, 16, 16, 16, 16, 16, artificial sections of hemp, grass, or plaster used as a substitute for the natural body. *Fig.* 2. A, nut; B, cap; C, thread.

PLATE X. SKELETON OF A GROUSE, OR PRAIRIE HEN (*Cupidonia cupido*, Baird), showing the different bones, as follows : — a, the skull; b, vertebra of the neck; c, humerus; d, forearm; f, phalanges; g, furcula; h, sternum; i, marginal indentations; j, thigh; k, tarsus; y, tibia; m, rump; n, coccygus; A, ribs; B, lower joint of thigh.

PART I.

DIRECTIONS

FOR COLLECTING, PRESERVING, AND MOUNTING

BIRDS, MAMMALS, FISHES,

ETC., ETC., ETC.

PART I.

CHAPTER I.

COLLECTING AND PRESERVING BIRDS.

SECTION I. *How to collect.* — Personal experience is a good, and in fact the only adequate, teacher we can have in learning any art. The need of such a teacher is felt by none more than by the naturalist who wishes to bring together a complete collection of the birds of even his own immediate district. Hence I trust I shall not be accused of egotism, if, in this section, I endeavor to impart to the reader some things that experience has taught me.

It is of first importance for the collector to gain as complete a knowledge as possible of the notes and habits of birds, and of the localities frequented by those he wishes to procure. This knowledge may be gained by carefully studying the writings of men who have paid particular attention to the subject. *Too* much dependence must not be placed on books, as the best of these contain error as well as truth ; besides, birds are very variable in their habits in different localities. The collector must then depend mainly upon himself. He must visit *every* locality, — the mountain top and the dark swampy thicket, as well as the meadow, the plain, or the open forest, as in each of these localities he will find species that he may no, meet elsewhere. A little patience will help any one through the worst of places.

The quaking bog, where a misstep may plunge the adventurer into the slimy ooze, is also an excellent locality for

certain species. But when the collector returns home wet
and hungry, fatigued and disheartened, — as he now and
then will, — let him not be discouraged. Try again! the
next day, and even the next, if need be, until the desired
specimen is obtained. After all, the earnest naturalist will
be amply rewarded for the exercise of patience and perseverance by securing a rare specimen.

The *true* naturalist never thinks of cold and disappoint-
ment, of days of fatigue and hours of patient watching,
when at last he holds in his hand the long-searched-for
bird. Ample reward is this for all his former trials; he is
now ready to go into bog and through brier. And thus the
enthusiastic naturalist travels on, not discouraged by toil
and trouble, laughed to scorn by the so-called "practical"
men, who are unable to appreciate his high motive. This,
however, he forgets when in field or study he meets with
the cordial greeting of his brother naturalist, as they with
mutual interest relate their discoveries and adventures.

To the travelling collector a few special hints are necessary. While visiting a remote region, but little known,
one should not neglect to shoot numbers of every bird met
with, even if they are common species at home, as they
will not only furnish data on the distribution of the species,
but they may present interesting characters peculiar to
that locality. If a certain species appears common, do not
delay collecting specimens, for peculiar circumstances may
have brought them together in unusual numbers; at some
future time they may be rare.

A well-trained dog is of great value while collecting
birds, especially the Quails, Marsh Wrens, Sea-side and
Sharp-tailed Finches, — in fact, all birds that are difficult to
start in open meadows and grassy places. While searching thickets, great watchfulness should be observed, especially in the autumn, when many birds have no conspicuous
note, otherwise many of the more wary of the Warblers

will escape notice. The slightest chirp should be carefully followed; the slightest motion of the branches closely watched. If a bird is seen that is not fully recognized, it should be shot at once, for in no other way can it be determined whether it is not a *rara avis.*

By carefully watching the motions of birds, the collector will soon become so expert as to be able generally to distinguish the different species of Warblers, even at a distance. Carefully scrutinize also the tops of tall forest-trees, as I have there taken, in autumn, some of the rarest Warblers.

In spring male birds are quite readily found, as they are then in full song; but the same caution must be used in collecting females that is practised in autumn, as they are generally shy and difficult to find. Hence it is a good rule always to secure the female *first*, when she is seen with the male; for, in spite of all the collector's efforts, he will find that there will be four males to one female in his collection.

During winter some birds may be found in the thick woods that one would hardly expect to find at this season, such as the Robin, Golden-winged Woodpecker, etc. The open fields should not be neglected even during snow-storms, as it is then that such ordinarily cautious birds as the Snowy Owl may be approached quite readily; or the capture of a Jerfalcon may reward the collector for a disagreeable tramp. The salt marshes and sandy sea-shores are the resort of a great many winter birds, and the collector will perhaps find himself amply repaid for a few visits to these localities at this season.

Do not neglect to collect the young of birds; by procuring specimens of these from the time they become fully fledged until they attain the perfectly mature plumage, one becomes familiar with all the stages through which a given species passes, and will thus avoid many errors into which some of our eminent ornithologists have fallen, —

that of mistaking the young of certain well-known birds for a different species from the adult, from not being acquainted with the immature stages. All birds should be taken that exhibit any unusual characters, such as unusually large or small bills or feet; or change of plumage, such as very pale, or very bright, cases of albinism, etc.

The gun used by a collector should have a small bore, not larger than No. 14, for shooting small birds; for Ducks, and other large water-birds, one of larger calibre will be found more effectual. The best shot to use for small birds is "Dust shot," if it can be procured; if not, No. 12 will answer. No. 8 will do for Ducks and large birds. For Hawks and Eagles, Ealy's wire cartridges are the best.

In shooting small birds, load as lightly as possible. Put in no more shot than is required to kill the bird. As you can approach very near most small birds, you will find, by experiment, that you can kill them with very little shot. If too much powder is used, it will impel the shot with so much force as to send it completely through the bird, thereby making *two* holes, when less powder, by causing less force, would have made only *one*, and the bird would have been killed just as effectually. When shot goes into the body of a bird, it generally carries feathers with it, and in a measure plugs the hole; but when it is forced through and comes out, it often carries away a small patch of feathers and skin, leaving an open wound, from which the blood flows freely.

If the bird is not instantly killed by shooting, the thumb and forefinger should be placed with a firm pressure on each side of its body under the wings, when it will soon die. This operation compresses the lungs and prevents the bird's breathing. Besides mercifully ending its suffering, its death causes the flow of blood in a great measure to cease, for this reason it should be killed as quickly as possible.

The mouth, nostrils, and vent should now be plugged with cotton or tow. By blowing aside the feathers the shot-holes may be detected; if they bleed, or are in the abdomen or rump, a pinch of calcined plaster * should be placed upon them; this absorbs the blood, or any fluid that may ooze out. When shot enters either the abdomen or rump, it is apt to cut the intestines and set free the fluids contained therein. If the blood has already soiled the feathers, remove as much as is possible with a knife, then sprinkle plaster on the spot, and rub the soiled feathers gently between the thumb and fingers; this, if repeated, will generally remove any spots of blood, etc., if the operation is performed before the blood becomes dry. When the blood is dry, it is removed after the bird is skinned, as will be hereafter described.

Next make a note of the color of the eyes, feet, and bill of the specimens, also note the color of the cere in birds of prey, and the naked skin of the lores and about the bill of the Herons, also about the heads of the Vultures. After smoothing the feathers carefully, place the bird in a paper cone,† head first, then pin or twist up the larger end, taking care not to injure the tail-feathers. The blood can be washed from the feathers of all the swimmers, but the bird, in this case, should be allowed to dry before packing in paper. If grease or oily matter has oozed out upon the feathers, the bird should not be washed, but the plaster be used as before, only in larger quantities.

All traces of blood should be instantly removed from white feathers, as it is very apt to stain them if it remains upon them long. The paper containing the bird should

* This is burned plaster or gypsum, and is used by stucco-makers. If it cannot be procured, the unburned plaster or common ground gypsum used by farmers, or air-slacked lime, pulverized chalk, or ashes, — in fact, anything that will absorb the blood, — will answer.

† The leaves of an old pamphlet are about the right size for making cones for small birds, and can be easily obtained.

be placed in a light basket, — a willow fish-basket is the best for this purpose, — suspended by a strap over the shoulder, and resting upon the hip. If there are but one or two birds in the basket, it should be filled with grass, or loose paper, to keep them steady, as otherwise they might receive injury by rolling from side to side. In packing birds, avoid putting the largest at the top, as their weight will cause the smallest to bleed. Do not hold a bird in the hand any longer than is necessary ; if possible, take it by the feet or bill, for the perspiration from the hand tends to impair the gloss of the plumage.

A good collector must practise, in order to become a good shot. He must always keep his gun in readiness, for at any moment a bird that he desires may start up at his feet, or peer out from the bushes for only an instant before flying away; by being ready, he will thus secure many birds that he would otherwise lose.

To be in readiness at all times, the gun should be carried in the hollow of the left arm, with the muzzle pointed backwards, or with the stock under the right arm, with the muzzle pointed towards the ground, which is undoubtedly the safest way, especially if you are hunting with a companion. Too much caution cannot be used in handling a loaded gun, especially by a professional collector, who may spend two thirds of his time with a gun in his hand. A gun should never be carried in other than three ways, — the two above mentioned and directly over the shoulder. If the collector becomes accustomed to these ways, which are all perfectly safe, he will never think of any other. Surely, this caution is necessary to one who is travelling through all sorts of places, when a slip or a fall with a carelessly held gun might cripple him for life, by an accidental discharge.

While passing through thick bushes, *always* carry the gun under the arm, as this prevents its accidental discharge by the bushes catching the trigger or hammer. Never allow the muzzle of the gun to point at any one, even for an instant. All these things depend upon habit, and will cause a thoughtful man, who has handled a gun for a long time, to be much more careful than a person who seldom takes one in his hands. The thoughtful man prefers rather to avoid accidents to himself and others — by care in advance — than to risk the chance of having to mourn his carelessness afterwards. The various devices for snaring birds are undoubtedly the best ways to secure them without injuring their plumage. But the collector will have to rely mainly upon his gun ; and by following the above instruction regarding the light charges, he will find that he will generally kill a bird without injuring its plumage seriously. If he carefully attends to it afterward in the way described, he will save himself much trouble when he wishes to preserve it.

In an old French cook-book may be found a receipt for a rabbit-stew, commencing with, " First, catch your rabbit," etc., — which rule is applicable to the collector. First, study with attention the art of collecting. Many and long have been the lessons in collecting that I have taken in long tramps through sunshine and storm, in the bracing air among the mountains of Northern Maine and New Hampshire, on sandy islands and rocky shores, amid the luxuriant forests and along the rivers and lagoons of semi-tropical Florida. Hours of danger and perplexity have been mingled with days of inexpressible pleasure, which all must experience who study from the Great Book of Nature. Not easily, then, I may add, have I learned what I am trying to impart to others in these pages.

Since writing the preceding, I have been informed by my friend, Mr. W. Brewster, of Cambridge, that in collecting such small birds as the Warblers, Sparrows, Wrens, etc., he has used a "blow-gun" to great advantage, constructed

1*

somewhat after the pattern of the celebrated instrument that is used by the natives of some portions of South America to shoot poisoned arrows. His "gun" is made of pine-wood, and is about four feet and a half long; it is bored smoothly the whole length with a quarter-inch hole. For ammunition Mr. Brewster uses balls made of soft putty. These, blown at birds, will hit them hard enough to kill, if the gun be aimed rightly, which art can be acquired by practice. This is certainly the preferable way to collect small birds, as it does the plumage no harm. I would suggest, however, that a tube of thin brass be used in place of wood; if it were longer, say six feet, it would carry with greater force and more accuracy. Glass would be still better, if it could be supported by wood to prevent breakage, as it would be much smoother. The balls of putty should be made to fit moderately tight. I have never tried this method myself, but Mr. Brewster has, in a satisfactory manner, as described above. I only wait an opportunity to test them myself, and trust that others will do the same.

SECTION II. *How to prepare Specimens. Instruments, Materials, etc.** — The instruments needed in preserving birds and mammals are: a pair of common pliers, Plate I. Fig. 1; a pair of cutting pliers, Fig. 2; a pair of tweezers, Fig. 3; a scalpel, Fig. 4; two brushes, — one soft, the other stiff; a flat file, and needles and thread.

The materials needed are: wire of annealed iron of sizes between 26 and 10, also some very fine copper wire; common thread, coarse and fine, also some very fine, soft thread from the cotton-factories, — this is wound on what are called "bobbins"; it is used in the manufacture of cloth, — cotton tow or hemp, and fine grass; for the latter the long tough kind that grows in the woods is the best.

* All the instruments and the wire may be procured at the hardware stores in the cities or larger towns.

Fig. 8

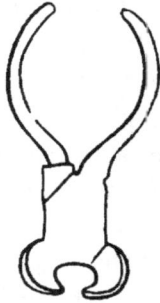

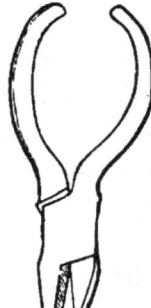

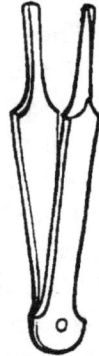

Fig. 2

Fig. 1

Fig. 3

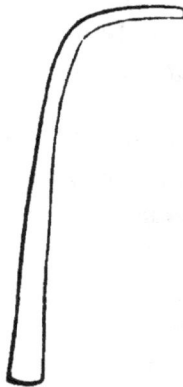

Fig. 5

Fig. 7

Fig. 4

Fig. 6

Plate I

Arsenic is the best substance that can be used in preserving skins, and the only one necessary. Other preparations
are no better, and often much *worse*. Strange as it may appear to some, I would say avoid especially all the so-called
arsenical soaps; they are at best but filthy preparations;
beside, it is a fact to which I can bear painful testimony,
that they are — especially when applied to a greasy skin —
poisonous in the extreme. I have been so badly poisoned,
while working upon the skins of some fat water-birds that
had been preserved with arsenical soap, as to be made
seriously ill, the poison having worked into the system
through some small wounds or scratches on my hands.
Had pure arsenic been used in preparing the skins the
effect would not have been as *bad*, although grease and
arsenic are generally a blood poison in *some* degree; but
when combined with "soap," the effect — at least, as far as
my experience goes — is much more injurious.

Arsenic alone will *sometimes* poison *slightly* the wound
with which it comes in contact, but no more than common salt. There will be a slight festering and nothing
more; but, on the contrary, when combined with fat, a
poison is generated that must be carefully guarded against.
It sometimes works under the nails of the fingers and
thumbs, while one is at work skinning (especially if the
birds are fat). Rubber cots should be put upon the fingers
or thumbs the instant the slightest wound is detected,
whereby much pain may be avoided at a small cost. The
cots alluded to can be procured of almost any druggist for
ten cents each.

Arsenic, however, cannot be used with too great care,
as it is a deadly poison. In no case should it be left in
the way of children. I have a drawer, wide, long, and
shallow, in the bench at which I work upon birds, where
my arsenic is kept safely, and it is always accessible. But
there is probably not so much danger attending the use

of pure dry arsenic as people generally suppose. I have been told repeatedly, by competent physicians, that the small quantity taken, either by inhalation while using it, or by numerous other accidental ways, would be beneficial, rather than injurious; but be that as it may, I have used dry arsenic constantly for ten years, and have not yet, I think, experienced any injurious effects from it. It must be remembered that I have, of course, used it carefully. When used with care, in the ordinary manner, it is undoubtedly the safest and the best material that can be used in preparing skins for the cabinet. I have never yet had a skin decay, or attacked by moths, that was well preserved by the use of arsenic. Arsenic is very cheap, varying from five to ten cents per pound by the wholesale, and retailed at twenty-five cents by druggists, but when bought by the ounce the price is enormous.

There is, however, another poison to which one is exposed while skinning animals, which cannot be too carefully guarded against, for it is much more injurious in its effects than fat and arsenic. I speak of the animal poison that results from the first stage of decomposition. If on a warm day one skins birds from which an offensive odor arises, and a peculiar livid or purplish appearance of the skin upon the abdomen is seen, and the intestines are distended with an extremely poisonous gas, — which is the source of the offensive, sickening odor, — there is danger of being poisoned. When this gas is inhaled, or penetrates the skin through the pores (which are generally open on a warm day), a powerful and highly dangerous poison is apt to be the result.

In a few days numerous pimples, which are exceedingly painful, appear upon the skin of the face and other parts of the person, and upon those parts where there is a chafing or rubbing become large and deep sores. There is a general languor, and, if badly poisoned, complete prostration results; the slightest scratch upon the skin becomes a festering sore. Once poisoned in this manner (and I speak from experience), one is never afterwards able to skin any animal that has become in the *least* putrid, without experiencing some of the symptoms above described. Even birds that you handled before with impunity, you cannot now skin without great care.

The best remedy in this case is, as the Hibernian would say, not to get poisoned, — to avoid skinning all birds that exhibit the slightest signs of putrescence; this is especially to be guarded against in warm weather, and in hot climates, where I have seen a single hour's work upon putrid birds nearly prove fatal to the careless individual.

If you *get* poisoned, bathe the parts frequently in cold water; and if chafed, sprinkle the parts, after bathing, with wheat flour. These remedies, if persisted in, will effect a cure, if not too bad; then, medical advice should be procured without delay.

It is just as easy to skin fresh birds as putrid ones, and much pleasanter, and in this way the evil will be avoided. If it is necessary to skin a putrid bird, — as in the case of a rare specimen, — a good bath of the hands and face in clear, cold water will entirely prevent the poison from taking effect, provided the skinning is not protracted too long. But generally, if the bird is putrid, I would advise the collector to throw it away, and obtain others that are safer to skin.

If birds and mammals are injected, by means of a small glass syringe, with a small quantity of carbolic acid at the mouth and vent, it will prevent decomposition from taking place immediately. After injecting, the mouth and vent should be plugged to prevent the acid from staining the feathers. Birds injected in this way for three successive days will continue fresh for a long time, and, if kept in a dry place, will harden completely without decomposing.

They may afterwards be skinned, as will be described hereafter. Impure carbolic acid will answer as well as the
refined, and it is much cheaper.

The cost of this acid is trifling, and it will often prove
beneficial in preserving birds in warm weather when they
cannot be skinned immediately. But I would not advise
its use in preserving birds when it can possibly be avoided,
as it dulls the plumage, and is offensive in its odor in connection with the juices of the birds while they are being
skinned. It is, perhaps, needless to add that this acid
is a dangerous internal poison; it also burns the skin
badly when allowed to come in contact with it, but all
injurious effects may be removed by applying oil to the
spot.

As a collector walks much, he must have something on
his feet that is easy and at the same time serviceable. I
have found that in stony countries like New England the
best things are canvas shoes that lace up in front, tightly
about the ankles and over the instep, to prevent slipping up
and down, which is the worst possible thing that could
happen while on a long tramp ; the soles should be broad,
so that the toes may have room enough without crowding.
With such shoes I have found that I could walk farther
than with anything else, and be less wearied in the end.
If the feet are wet from walking in water, with canvas
shoes on them they will soon dry, as the water will all run
out upon walking a short time on dry ground. Anything
that is water-proof will be much too heavy to travel in,
besides being injurious to the feet.

In sandy localities, or on marshes, or in winter when the
snow covers the ground, Indian moccasons are the easiest
and best things that can possibly be worn ; but in stony
places they are not of sufficient thickness to protect the
feet from receiving injury from the hard surface, otherwise they are exceedingly easy. They are not water-proof,

so that unless the snow is frozen in winter they are of no use. These moccasons can be procured almost anywhere in Maine and New Hampshire, and sometimes in Boston. They are manufactured mostly in Canada. For clothes, perhaps the best that can be worn in summer is a suit of fine canvas of some dark color, to correspond with the foliage; in winter, white, to correspond with the snow; in both cases the wearer is less conspicuous, and can approach his game much more readily. This cloth will not wear out or tear easily, and is every way fitted for travelling in the woods.

I would next call attention to making stands on which to put birds after they have been mounted, as one of the necessities of the cabinet. Simple stands in the form of the letter T (Plate VIII. Fig. 3, f) are generally wanted. Any carpenter can make them. Different sizes will be needed, from one with the standard two inches high with a cross-piece one inch long, to a foot standard with a six-inch cross-piece, with bottoms to match. If made of pine, these stands may be painted white. of a very pure unchanging color, in the following manner. Buy white zinc at thirty cents per pound, and nice frozen glue at from twenty-five to thirty cents per pound; dissolve the glue thoroughly in hot water, then strain; to a pint and a half of water use a quarter of a pound of glue, to this add one pound of zinc, stir well, with the vessel that contains it in boiling water, then, with a brush, apply to the stands; put on two coats. If the paint has a yellowish cast, put in a few drops of bluing; it will change it at once. Thus you will find that you have a nice white coat of paint that will remain unchanged longer than oil colors. Any other color can be used, if preferred, in the same manner.

Fancy stands are made in the following way. For mossy stands, select a wooden bottom of suitable shape and size, — those with the edges bevelled are generally used, — and with the pliers force a piece of wire into it in the centre, then bend the wire in imitation of a branch or small tree, then wind it with hemp to give it the required shape; additional wires may be fastened on to represent the smaller twigs.

The whole is now to be covered with a coating of glue, and sprinkled with pulverized moss, or small pieces of moss are placed upon it smoothly. If the work is performed neatly, a perfect imitation of a little tree will be the result, upon which the bird is placed. If artificial leaves are to be used, they may be placed upon the twigs with glue.

If, instead of a wire, a twig bent in the required form can be procured, and fastened to the bottom with wire, it may be covered with moss without winding with hemp. The fancy stands seen with dealers in birds are generally made of a substance called *papier-maché*, that is, manufactured of paper pulp and glue as follows: Tear paper in small pieces and place it in water, let it stand overnight. Then, as it will be entirely soaked, reduce it to a perfect pulp, either by forcing it through a sieve or by stirring it. When reduced to a pulp, drain the water away. Dissolve a quarter of a pound of glue in a pint of water; mix with this a pint of pulp, heat it, and stir it well; then it is ready for use. Prepare a stand as described. Mould the pulp upon it in any shape to suit the fancy. It should have the consistency of putty, in order to work well. If it is too thin, put in more of the pulp: if too dry, more water.

With this substance you can imitate almost anything in the shape of miniature trees, with hollows, knots, crooked limbs, etc. By drawing over the whole, when finished, a comb, the bark of a tree can be imitated exactly. When perfectly dry, the limbs of the tree can be painted brown in the manner described. The bottom of the stand is

B

painted green, and sprinkled with a substance resembling green sand, called " smolt," which may be procured at the painter's ; over this is sometimes sprinkled thin glass, broken fine, which is called " frosting," and is also used by painters.

Rocks can be imitated well with *papier-maché*. If studded with small pieces of quartz the effect is heightened; they then may be painted in imitation of granite, sandstone, etc. The sandstone is easily imitated by sprinkling on sand before the pulp is dry. There are many other things that may be imitated with this wonderful substance, but, having given the preceding hints, I leave the reader to experiment at his leisure upon them.

For the scientific cabinet I would advise the use of the plain white stands as being much neater. The others are only fit for ornament.

One other thing is necessary. Take a thin board, and at intervals of two inches tack transversely strips of wood (Plate IV. Fig. 1); then cut a strip of paper as wide as the board, and with glue make it adhere at the top of the strips and at the middle of the intervening space, so as to form a corrugated appearance (Fig. 2). These are used in drying skins of birds. Each board should have about twelve such spaces, varying in width from two to four inches, the boards varying in width from four inches to one foot. These boards, with careful use, will last a long time.

SECTION III. *Measuring, Skinning, and Preserving Birds.* — For measuring, a pair of dividers, or compasses, a steel rule, divided into hundredths of an inch, and a longer rule, divided into inches and half-inches, will be wanted. To measure the bird, proceed as follows : Place the bird upon its back upon the longer rule, with the end of the tail at the end of the rule; the neck is stretched at full length, without straining; the bill must be pointed with

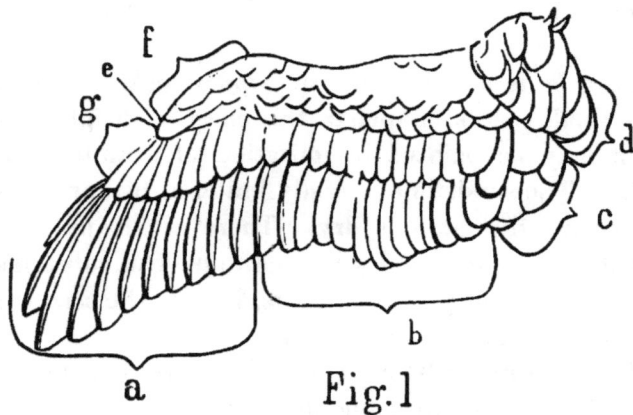

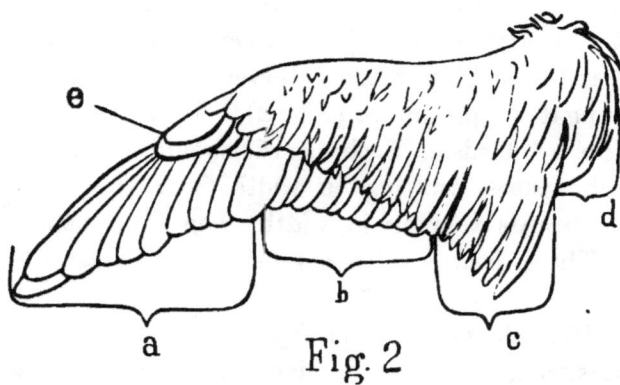

Fig. 1

Fig. 2

Plate II.

the rule. Record the number of inches upon a strip of paper; if there is a fractional part of an inch, measure it with the dividers, and find how many hundredths it contains upon the smaller rule, and record it. This is "the length of the bird."

Stretch the wings out to the full length, with the bird still upon its back; measure these from tip to tip as "the stretch of wing." Measure the wing from the tip to the carpel joint, or bend, with the dividers (Plate X. d), for "the length of the wing." The tail is to be measured — also with the dividers — from the tip to the root for "the length of the tail." Measure the tarsus (Plate VII. g) as "the length of the tarsus." Measure the bill, from the tip of the upper mandible to the base (if the base is not well defined, as in the Ducks, measure to the feathers); this is "the length of bill along the culmen" (Plate III. h). Measure from the tip of the upper mandible to the gape (e) for "the length from gape"; also from the tip of the lower mandible to the angle of the gonys (s) for "the length of gonys" (c). In the Hawks, measure to the cere.

The color of the eyes, feet, and bill is now observed and recorded, also the date of collection and the locality in which the bird was collected. If the bird is in worn plumage, the fact should be recorded, as this will affect the measurements; also if it is moulting or in perfect plumage. As the records now made are only temporary, signs may be used to save time, such as X—— would denote an adult bird in perfect plumage, Y|—— would denote a young bird in worn plumage, YY|——| would denote a young bird not a year old and moulting, —this stage in the life of the bird is called the "young-of-the-year." By using some such signs as these much time will be saved. When the collector becomes expert at measuring, he will find that all small birds can be measured and recorded in

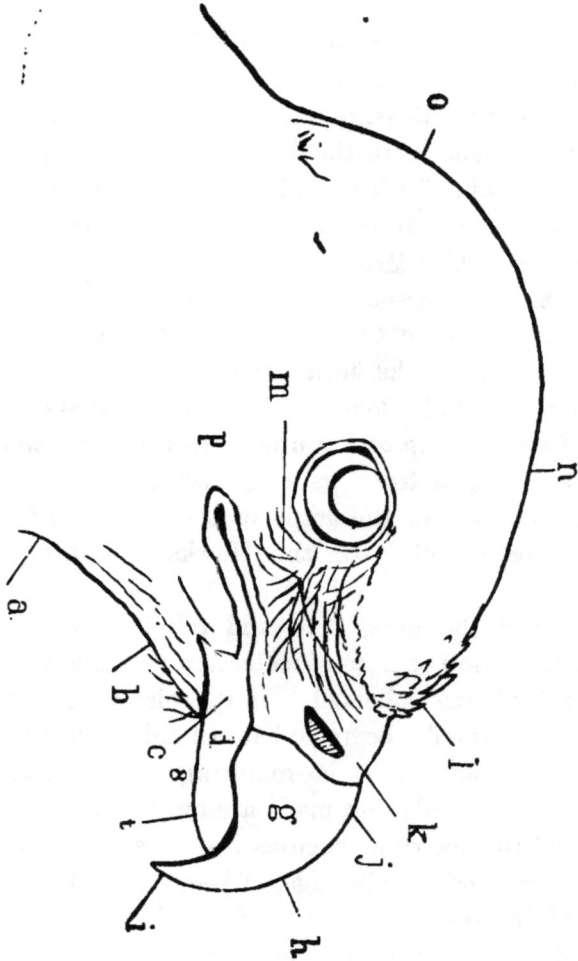

Plate III

about three minutes, and the larger ones in a little longer time.

Skinning. — First, have plenty of plaster near at hand. Remove the cotton from the mouth and vent, and place a fresh plug in the mouth alone. The method now about to be described is one that will apply to all birds, excepting those to be hereafter named.

Place the bird upon its back; with the forefinger and thumb part the feathers on the abdomen, and a bare longitudinal space will be discovered, extending from the breast to the vent. With the scalpel divide the skin in the centre of this bare space, commencing at the lower part of the breast-bone, or sternum (Plate X. o), and ending at the vent. Now peel the skin off to the right and left, and sprinkle plaster upon the exposed abdomen. Force the leg on the right side up *under* the skin, at the same time drawing the skin down until the joint (p) appears; cut through this joint and draw the leg out as far as the tarsus or first joint (k); with the point of the knife sever the tendons on the lower part of the leg, then by a single scraping motion upwards they may all be removed, completely baring the bone; treat the other leg in a like manner, leaving both turned out as they were skinned. Place the finger under the rump near the tail, then with the scalpel cut through the backbone just in front of the coccygus (n) entirely through the flesh to the skin, — the finger beneath is a guide to prevent cutting the skin. This may be done very quickly after long practice, and there is no danger of severing the skin if proper care be used. Put on a fresh supply of plaster. Now grasp the end of the backbone firmly between the thumb and forefinger, and with the other hand pull the skin down on all sides towards the head, until the joint of the wing, where the last bone, or humerus (r), is joined to the body, appears; sever the bones at this joint, and draw the skin down over the neck and head. When the ears appear, with the thumb-nail remove the skin that adheres closely to the skull without breaking it, pull down to the eyes, then cut the skin off close to the eyelids, taking care not to cut or injure them; but be sure and cut close enough to remove the nictating membrane, as it will otherwise cause trouble. Skin well down to the base of the bill. Remove the eye with the point of the knife by thrusting it down at the side between the eye and the socket, then with a motion upward it can be removed without breaking; cut off enough of the back part of the skull to remove the brains easily. Proceed to skin the wings; draw them out until the forearm (Plate X. d) appears, to which the secondaries are attached; with the thumb-nail detach them by pressing downward forcibly. Remove the muscles and tendons — as explained on the leg — to the joint, where the forearm joins the humerus (B), then divide, removing the humerus entirely.

Now open the drawer containing the arsenic, and with a small flat piece of wood cover the skin completely with it; be sure that the cavities from which the brains and eyes were removed are filled. Take up the skin and shake it gently. The arsenic that remains adhering to it is sufficient to preserve it, provided the skin is damp enough; if not, it may be moistened slightly. Now fill the eye-holes * with cotton, tie the wing-bones with thread, as near together as the back of the bird was broad, then turn the skin back into its former position. Smooth the feathers of the head and wings with the fingers. With a few strokes of the feather duster, holding the skin up by the bill, remove the plaster and arsenic that may be adhering to the feathers.

If there is blood upon the feathers, it may be removed — if there is not much of it, and if it is dry — with the

* By which I mean the holes occupied by the eyes in the skull.

stiff brush by continuous brushing, assisted by scraping with the thumb-nail. A living bird cleans blood from its plumage by drawing each feather separately through its beak, thereby *scraping* off the blood ; the thumb-nail performs the part of the bill. If much bloody, with a soft sponge and water, wash away *all* traces of blood ; then throw plaster upon the wet spot, and remove it before it has time to harden or "set." By repeating this operation, at the same time lifting the feathers so as to allow the plaster to dry every part, and by using the soft brush, the feathers will soon dry. In this way any stains may be removed.

If the plumage is greasy, wash it with warm water and strong soap long enough to remove *every particle* of fatty matter that adheres to the feathers ; then rinse *thoroughly* in *warm* water, afterwards in cold. Be sure and remove all traces of the soap before putting on the plaster to dry, as the soap will be changed by the plaster into a gummy substance, which will be *very* difficult to remove.

After smoothing the feathers carefully, place the skin upon its back. With the tweezers take up a small roll of hemp or cotton, as large round and as long as the neck of the body that was taken out, and place it in the neck of the skin, taking care that the throat is well filled out ; then, by grasping the neck on each side with the thumb and finger, the hemp or cotton may be held in place, and the tweezers withdrawn. After placing the wings in the same position as the bird would have them when at rest, with the bones of the forearm pushed well into the skin, — so that they may lie down each side, and not cross each other, — with a needle and thread sew through the skin and the first quill of the primaries by pushing the needle through the skin on the *inside* and through the quill opposite, but be sure that the wing is in the proper place. (If it is too far forward, the feathers of the sides of the breast, that ought to lie smoothly over the bend of the wing, will be forced up and backward. If the wing is placed too far *back*, there will be a bare spot upon the side of the neck, — caused by the wing-coverts, which help, in connection with the feathers of the back, to hide the spot, being drawn either down or back too far. If the wing is placed too low, the same spot is seen, only it is elongated and extends along the back between the secondaries and feathers of the back ; if too high, the feathers of the back will appear pushed up, and will not lie smooth for obvious reasons. When the wing is in the right position, the feathers of the wing-coverts and back will blend nicely and smoothly, and the feathers of the sides of the breast will lie smoothly over the bend of the wing ; the ends of the closed quills will lie flat upon the tail, or nearly so.) Now draw the thread through so that but an inch is visible inside the skin, then push the needle through the skin from the outside just *below* the quill that it came out through, draw the thread through. and tie to the projecting end, thereby fastening the wing firmly to the side ; proceed in this way with the other wing.

Roll up loosely an oblong body of cotton or hemp of the same size as the body taken out, place it in the skin neatly, then draw the edges of the skin together where the incision was made, and sew them once in the centre ; tie the ends of the thread together. Take care to put the needle through the *edge* of the skin so as not to disturb the feathers. Smooth the feathers on the abdomen. Cross the feet upon the tail (Plate IV. Fig. 3), — which is spread slightly, — then place tne skin upon its back in the rounded places of the drying-board, spoken of on page 18 (Fig. 1, d), taking care that the feathers of the back are perfectly smooth. This rounded bed gives the back a natural rounded appearance, which cannot be made easily in any other way. Place the head with the

2

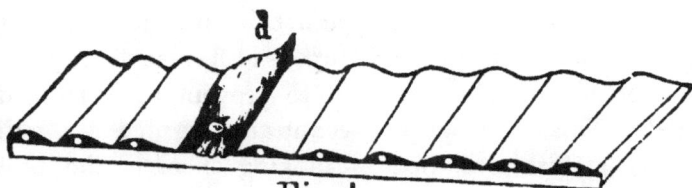

Fig 1

Fig. 2

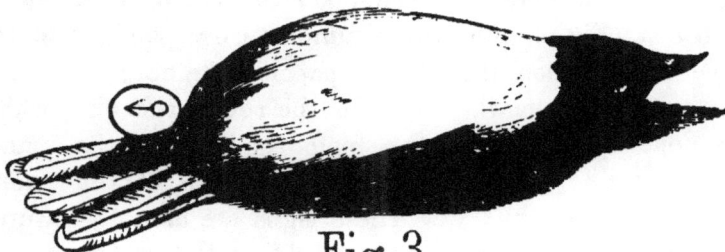

Fig. 3

Plate IV.

bill horizontal with the back or bottom of the rounded space, with the culmen (Plate IV., Fig. 1, d) nearly touching the paper. The skin must remain in this position without being disturbed until perfectly dry, which in very warm weather, with small birds, will be in about twenty-four hours.

If this corrugated board cannot be procured, the skin may be placed on its back upon a flat surface, with a little cotton on each side of it to prevent its getting displaced. This is what is technically termed "a skin" (Fig. 3), and this method of making them is the best I have ever seen practised, and one that I have used for years as being the most expedient. The skins so made are less liable to injury, being stronger than some others, and are also very easily mounted. I have made in a single day, in the manner described, fifty skins, and with practice almost any one will be able to do the same; ten minutes being ample time for each, including the measuring.

Before the skin is placed upon the board, it should be labelled (Fig. 3, ♂) with a number corresponding to the one placed upon the slip of paper containing the measurements, etc., marked also for the sex of the bird, which is done by using for the male the sign of the planet Mars, thus ♂; for the female the sign of the planet Venus is used, thus ♀. These signs are used by naturalists throughout the scientific world, and it is best to become accustomed to them.

Determining the Sex. — The sex of the bird is determined, not by the plumage, which will sometimes set the student at fault by its changes, and *should never be trusted in determining the sex*, but by dissection, as follows : Take the body of the bird after it has been removed, and cut with the scalpel through the ribs (Plate X. A) on the sides of the abdomen, thereby exposing the intestines; raise

these gently with the point of the knife, and beneath them
will be seen the sexual organs, which are fully illustrated
in the following diagrams.

PLATE V., Fig. 2, is an adult male (♂) in the breeding
season. 1 shows the position of the lungs, 2 the peculiar yellowish glands, — in some birds bright yellow, in the
present case — that of a song sparrow (*Melospiza melodia*.
Baird) — they are yellowish white, which, being present
in both sexes, if not examined closely, may be easily mistaken, in the young female, for the testicles of the male.
3, 3, are the testicles, much enlarged in this, the breeding
season. The sex of a bird in this stage is easily determined.

PLATE VI., Fig. 1, is a young male (♂) in the young-
of-the-year plumage. The figures refer to the same parts
as explained in the preceding. It will be perceived that
the testicles (3) are much smaller. At different seasons,
the testicles vary in size between this and the preceding.
In some birds they are elongated, and black in color,
as in the Herons; but they always occupy the same positions so nearly as to be readily distinguished. The peculiar white glands (2) are in this instance very prominent,
but they are readily known in all birds by their being flat,
while the testicles are always spherical.

PLATE V., Fig. 1. This is an adult female (♀) in the
breeding season. 1, 1, are the same peculiar glands observed
in the males; 2 is the ovary, a mass of spheres at this
season quite yellow and prominent; 3 is the oviduct, or
egg-passage, much enlarged in the present case, as it always
is during the breeding season, when it assumes a thick,
swollen appearance, while at other times it is translucent,
much smaller, and resembles a narrow, whitish line, not
readily perceived.

PLATE VI., Fig. 2, is a young-of-the-year female in autumn. 1, 1, the same white glands that at this stage of the

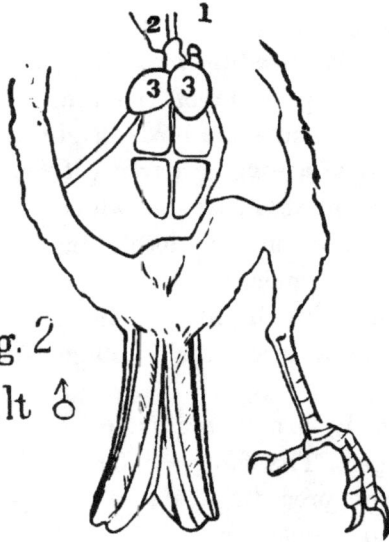

Fig. 2
Adult ♂

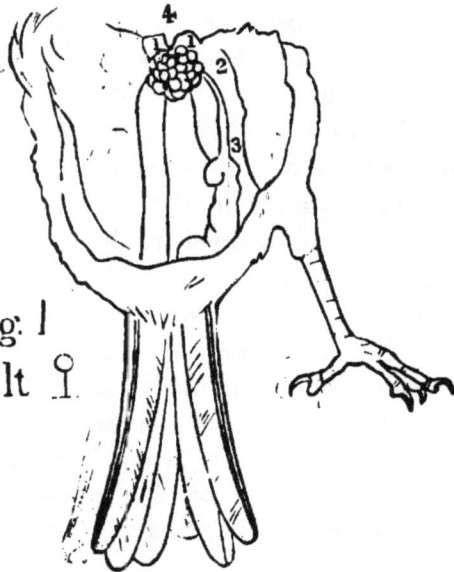

Fig. 1
Adult ♀

Plate V.

Fig. 2
Young ♀

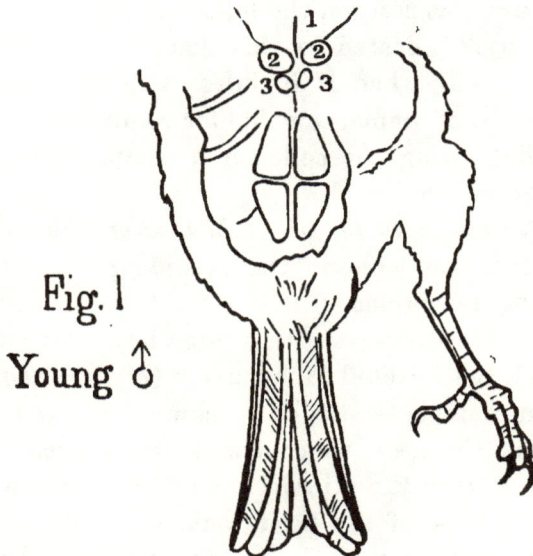

Fig. 1
Young ♂

Plate VI.

bird's life might at first sight be mistaken for the testicles of the male, but, upon looking closely the ovary (2) can be perceived, very small; upon applying a magnifying-glass it appears granular.

With these remarks and diagrams, I think any one with ordinary ability will, with a little practice, be able to determine this very important character in the scientific study of birds.

Contents of Stomach, etc. — The contents of the stomach must next be examined, which is done by opening the gizzard and crop. A little practice will enable the collector to state correctly what it contains, although the glass is sometimes necessary, as in the case of small birds. This is then recorded upon the slip of paper, which is put on file, to be copied into a book, in the following manner, — leaving a page, or, if the book is not wide enough, two pages, for each species, — first placing the *scientific* name at the head, as seen on the following page.

A book prepared in this manner, carefully indexed and paged, will, when it is filled with the measurements of birds, be of immense value for comparative measurements, besides giving the collector a complete history of each of his specimens.

Exceptions to the usual Method of Skinning. — All birds are to be prepared in the preceding manner, with the following exceptions.

All Woodpeckers with a large head and small neck — of which the Pileated Woodpecker (*Hylotomus pileatus*, Baird) is an example — should be skinned in the same manner as far as the neck, which should be severed, as it is impossible to turn the skin over the head; cut through the skin on the back of the head, making a longitudinal insertion of an inch or more, and draw the head through this. It should be carefully sewn up after the skin is turned back. Such specimens, when laid out to dry, should have the

Sialia sialis.

No	Date	Locality	Age	State of Plumage	Sex	Length	Stretch of Wing	Wing	Tail	Bill	Tarsus	Color of Eyes.	Color of Bill.	Color of Feet.	Contents of Stomach.	Remarks.
1022	1868 July 22	Newton, Mass	Young-of-year	Perfect	♂	7.00	12.45	3.20	2.56	.50	.82	Brown	Black	Black	Beetles and Flies	Spotted on breast.
1023	"	"	Adult	Worn	♀	7.00	12.00	3.95	2.40	.52	.62	"	"	"	Beetles	Shot in a field.
1934	Dec. 30	Jacksonville, Fl.	"	Perfect	♂	7.00	12.30	4.00	2.75	.49	.80	"	"	"	Berries	Shot on the Pine Barrens.
1969	1869. Jan. 3	"	"	"	♀	6.50	11.75	3.75	2.55	.50	.75	"	"	"	Seeds	Shot on the Pine Barrens.

head so placed that the bill is turned at right angles with the body, with the head resting on *one side*, and not on the *back* as before.

All Ducks with large heads should be skinned in the same way, with the exception that the insertion must be made *under* the head, on the throat. Ducks, Herons, Geese, large Sandpipers, and all other long-necked birds, should, when placed to dry, rest upon the *breast*, with the head and neck placed upon the back, and the head turned on one side. Herons with very long necks should have them bent once. The bill must be placed parallel with the neck and pointing forward.

While travelling it is not always convenient to fill out the bodies of large birds; it is better to pack them flat, with but little cotton in them, — just enough, however, to keep the opposite parts of the skin from coming in contact. The neck should *always* be filled. When it is impossible to procure stuffing for small birds, they may be packed flat also.

Birds that have been preserved with carbolic acid, even after they have been lying for years, and have become perfectly dry, may be skinned in the following manner: Place wet cotton or hemp under the wings, in the throat, and around the legs, and finally envelop the whole body in a thick coating. Place it in a close box, and let it remain a day or two until it is softened, then take it out and remove the skin as before directed; but more care will have to be exercised than in skinning fresh birds. Alcoholic specimens may be skinned; but the wet plumage had better be dried in the air without plaster. Mr. A. L. Babcock has a number of mounted birds in his collection at Sherborne, Massachusetts, that were preserved in alcohol, and sent from South America.

The beginner will find that some birds, such as the Cuckoos, Pigeons, and Doves, are very difficult to skin over

2 *   c

the rump without loosening the feathers; but this difficulty will be overcome by using particular care while skinning the spot that is tender. Some birds also have tender skin on the breast, and in such cases it almost always adheres so closely to the flesh that it is necessary to cut it away; this operation is somewhat tedious, but it is better than to risk tearing the skin by pulling it. An example of this is sometimes seen in the Wood Duck.

The best time to skin a bird is as soon as it is shot, when the muscles are relaxed, as the plumage is then in the best condition. In a short time the muscles become rigid, when it is extremely difficult to remove the skin; but the muscles soon relax again, and then you must skin *at once*, as this is the first stage — or the state immediately preceding the first stage — of decomposition. In very warm weather this rigidness of the muscles seldom occurs, then the bird rapidly decomposes. In warm weather, birds should be kept on ice until wanted; for if a bird remains only an hour in a warm room, or in the sun, it will sometimes spoil, especially if the blow-flies are allowed access to it. There is a species of blow-fly that is viviparous; I have seen such a fly alight upon a fresh bird, and, after introducing her ovipositor into the mouth of the specimen, exude an immense number of living, though minute, maggots. These maggots spread over the skin in all directions, moistening it with their slimy bodies, and soon render the specimen unfit for use by loosening the feathers.

It is difficult to remove the eggs of the common blow-fly when they are once placed upon the feathers. It is much better to prevent the flies from attacking specimens — which, if they are exposed during warm weather, they will do very quickly — by covering them, or placing them immediately upon ice.

SECTION IV. *Mounting Specimens.* — Almost any one

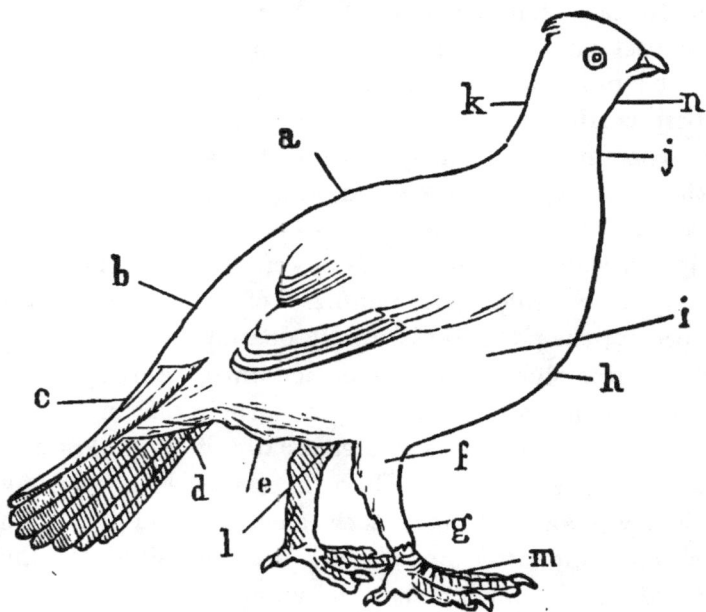

Plate VII.

can mount a bird, after receiving proper instruction ; but to make it look lifelike and natural requires constant and unceasing study of birds in their native haunts. The true art, then, can only be acquired by the earnest student of nature. The mere taxidermist, who constantly sits at his bench and works on birds without studying from nature, may acquire a certain degree of *skill*, but the attitudes of many of his stuffed birds will appear awkward and grotesque to the *naturalist*.

Therefore I say to those who would learn to mount birds in natural attitudes, *study nature.* Have all attitudes that every bird assumes engraved upon the brain, to be reproduced in the stuffed specimens ; from the one assumed by the delicate Warbler, that hops lightly from limb to limb, or swings gracefully from the topmost bough of some tall oak, to that of the mighty Eagle in his eager, downward swoop upon his trembling prey. Watch the screaming Gull in his almost innumerable positions upon the wing, the nimble Sandpiper running along the shore, and the gracefully floating Duck upon the water. After watching these in their various natural attitudes, work ; but do not cease to study for improvement, for the work of man is yet far from being *perfect.*

In mounting birds, skin as instructed in the preceding section, but do not tie the wing-bones together. Having cleaned and dusted the feathers, proceed to fill the neck to the natural size, without stretching, with " shorts," or the bran from wheat flour, or with hemp cut fine. Roll up some fine grass moderately hard in the shape of an oblong body (Plate VIII. Figs. 1, 2), then wind it smoothly with thread. This body should be of the same proportionate size as the one taken out, although not exactly of the same shape, for reasons that will be seen when the bird is mounted, but which cannot be easily explained. Have the body perfectly smooth, and the curves regular on every part.

Place the body inside the skin. Now cut wires of the right size (that is, large enough to support the bird when mounted; which can be learned by experience, although I would advise putting in as large wires as can be used without splitting the skin of the tarsi) and proper length for the wiring of the following parts : to go through the legs, for the neck, and for the tail. Straighten the wires by rolling them on the bench with a file, then sharpen them by holding the end obliquely against the edge of the bench and filing from you, at the same time twisting the wire; force the wire cut for the leg up through the sole of the foot, through the tarsus, along the leg-bone into the centre of the side of the grass body (Plate VIII. Fig. 1, a), through this so that the end will protrude for an inch; bend the end down in the form of an L (Fig. 1, b), and again force it into the body (Fig. 1, c), thereby clinching it so that it can have no motion whatever. The wire should protrude out of the sole at least two inches (Fig. 1, d).

Proceed in the same manner with the other leg; if this seems difficult at first, practice will soon overcome the difficulty. Be sure and clinch the wires *firmly*, as they will otherwise cause trouble. Force the wire cut for the head down through the skull near the base of the bill (Fig. 3, g) through the neck, — but it must not come out through the skin anywhere, — through the body (Fig. 1, e), out the other side, where it is clinched as before (Fig. 1, c). Force the wire cut for the tail through the bone left in the tail, and under the tail, into the body (Fig. 1, f); clinch as usual (Fig. 3, g). Bend the wire — which should protrude about two inches beyond the end of the tail — into the form of a T (Fig. 1, h); the cross-piece is placed about half the length of the tail; on this the tail rests. Pin up the incision by drawing the edges of the skin together and forcing pins through them into the body; then smooth the feathers over the place.

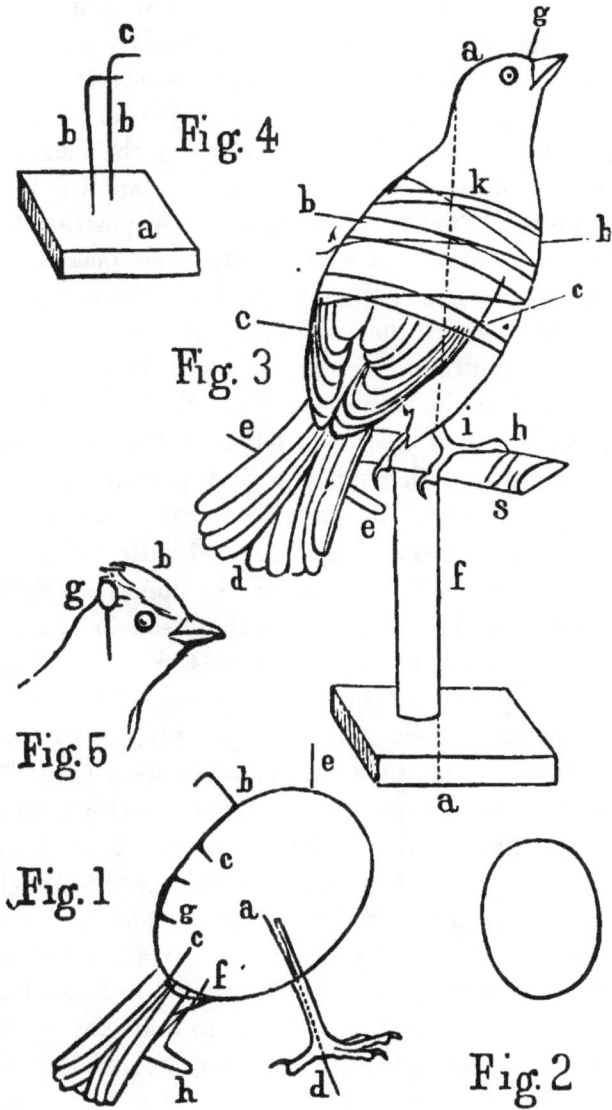

Fig. 4

Fig. 3

Fig. 5

Fig. 1

Fig. 2

Plate VIII.

Fasten the bird upon the stand by passing the wires of the feet through the holes in the cross-piece (Plate VIII. Fig. 3, h), then twist the ends of the wire around the ends of the cross-piece (Fig. 3, s) to fasten it firmly. Place the bird in position with the tarsi inclining backward (Fig. 3, i), so that a line dropped from the back of the head, passing through the body, would pass down the centre of the stand (Fig. 3, a, a). This is a natural rule, and one that applies to all perching birds. Next arrange the wings in position by applying the same rules that were given when making a skin ; in this case, however, the following additional rule may be of use. The end of the bone of the forearm should reach just half the length and width of the body where it meets the lower end of the thigh (see Plate X. B). Having arranged the wing, pin it near the bend to the body (Plate VIII. Fig. 3, b), also through the first primary quill (Fig. 3, c). The wings should in some cases be, placed at a little distance from the body, as is natural with the Thrushes, and some other species. This may be done by lengthening the second wire (Fig. 3, c). Put the head in the proper position, cut off the protruding wire (Fig. 3, g). Plait the tail-feathers by placing the inner web over the outer (Fig. 3, d); then place a piece of fine copper wire across the tail, and fasten it to the ends of the cross-piece (Fig. 3, e). Fix the artificial eyes in their proper position with glue or putty : then wind the bird with the fine cotton on the breast and shoulders and over the secondaries (Fig. 3, k); this is to keep the feathers smooth while it is drying.

To mount a bird with the wings extended, proceed as before explained, but raise the wings, and use longer wires to pin them in position. Then, to hold the quills and secondaries in place, bend a wire over the whole width of the wing, passing on each side of them. In skinning and mounting Ducks, open under the wing. This is accomplished by making an incision on the side, from the place where the humerus joins the sternum (Plate X. B) to just beyond the lower joint of the thigh (p), after which skin as before.

If any feathers become twisted or bent, they may be instantly straightened by holding them in steam. If the feathers are to be smoothed, raise them with the fingers or tweezers, and let them fall back in place; they will generally come down smoothly. If the feathers come out, put a drop of glue upon the end of each, and place it in the proper position; it will stay, when dry. In this way large bare places may be covered.

Mounting dried Skins. — To mount dried skins, remove the stuffing with which they are filled, and supply its place with dampened cotton, also wrap the legs well with it; place the skin in a box, where it must remain until it becomes pliable, but not too soft, as it is then liable to drop in pieces. It is to be mounted as described, excepting that the neck is filled with cut hemp instead of bran. Birds mounted from dried skins require more care in mounting, and more binding to bring the feathers into proper position, than fresh birds.

Never paint or varnish the feet or bill of a bird; the scales on the feet of birds are one of the most interesting characters in the study of ornithology, and they cannot readily be seen when covered with paint or varnish. In mounting birds larger than a Robin, the muscles of the leg-bone must be supplied by winding the tibia with hemp until the original size and shape is attained. Particular attention must be paid to the legs of the Waders and rapacious birds. The exceptions to this rule are all swimming birds; as the tibia is buried in the body, it does not need winding.

In mounting Humming-Birds with the wings extended, especially from dried skins, there is no need of wiring the leg. Place a single wire in the back part of the body, with

the point firmly clinched, and the end protruding back
from the abdomen for three or four inches. This wire will
sustain the bird. Always wire the feet in the usual way
if the bird is to be mounted in the attitude of rest. In
mounting other small birds, this method of wiring will answer when the bird is represented as flying. Large birds,
when mounted in the attitude of flying, should be wired
in the usual manner, with the wires that extend beyond
the soles of the feet cut short; then a wire is forced down
through the back and clinched under the body, with the
end pointing upward; cut off this end so that it will protrude but a half-inch beyond the skin, then bend it under
the feathers into the form of a hook or ring; to this fasten
a thread, and suspend the bird. To make the bird incline
downward, place the wire well back; upward, farther forward, or nearer the head. Fine copper wire will answer
to suspend large birds in this manner. In mounting a
bird in this position, with the wings fully extended, care
should be taken that they are properly arched.

While arranging the wings, it is not convenient to keep
the bird suspended, as it will not be sufficiently firm.
Sharpen two stout wires and fasten them at both ends
(Plate VIII. Fig. 4, b, b), perpendicularly in a block of
wood (a), parallel to each other, and about two inches
apart. These wires should be at least four inches long.
Bend about an inch and a half of the ends down, parallel
with the block (c). Force these ends into the abdomen of
the bird that is being mounted, and it will be firmly held
in place while the different parts are being arranged, after
which it can be suspended as described.

Sometimes it is necessary to mount the skins of rare
birds when they are badly decayed. To mount skins in
this condition requires skill and patience, as well as a knowledge of their different parts. The manner in which I have
mounted them is this: First, moisten the skin as de-

scribed, then make a body, as before, and place a wire of the proper size and length in the usual place for the neck, and wind it with hemp to the natural size; place the head, wings, feet, and tail in the proper position; then, after spreading glue upon the body, place each feather or piece of skin carefully in its proper place, commencing at the tail and working towards the head; when this is finished, bind the bird as usual.

Birds that have been mounted require at least ten days for the skin to dry before the thread is removed, which is done by cutting down the back with scissors, after which cut off all protruding wires, and unplait the tail-feathers and smooth them. To elevate the crest of a bird, or any other naturally elevated feathers, — such as the elongated feathers on the necks of some species of Grouse, etc., — roll a piece of cotton into a ball, and force a pin or piece of sharpened wire through it (Plate VIII. Fig. 5, g). Place this wire or pin in the bird in such a manner that the feathers to be elevated may rest on the cotton in a natural position (Fig. 5, b). After the skin becomes hardened the cotton may be removed, and the feathers will retain the desired position.

CHAPTER II.

COLLECTING AND PRESERVING MAMMALS.

SECTION I. *Collecting.*— Because mammals are not quite as interesting at first sight as birds, the study of this class of animals has been somewhat neglected; and but comparatively few naturalists are even aware of the existence of some of the smaller mammalia that live about them. They are, however, worthy of special attention, and, if studied, will soon be found particularly interesting.

In collecting mammals, excepting some of the larger species, the gun is of but little use; they must be taken almost entirely with traps. Shrews and Moles may be frequently found where they have been dropped by cats, who catch them, but do not eat them. In this way a great many valuable specimens may be obtained.

Another way to procure Mice and Shrews is to turn over old logs and stumps, under which these little animals frequently hide, and while dazzled by the light's coming in suddenly upon them, they may be readily seized in the hand. Mice may also be trapped.

Squirrels may be shot or caught in traps; Foxes, trapped, shot, or dug out of their holes. Woodchucks are easily trapped or dug out. Skunks are very disagreeable animals to handle, but when one once becomes accustomed to capturing them he can do it in perfect safety. The best way is to catch them in a "box-trap" baited with the head of a chicken; when caught, immerse trap and skunk in water until the animal is dead. Treated in this manner, they will not emit any of their disagreeable scent. By breaking the backbone with a stout stick, when the animal is caught in a steel trap, the disagreeable emission will be prevented. All animals should be killed either by breaking the backbone or by compressing the ribs, to stop the breath; *never* by a blow on the head, as this is liable to injure the skull, which must be preserved entire for scientific investigation.

The following animals may be decoyed into traps by means of peculiar scents: Foxes, Fishers, Martens, Minks, Weasels, Wildcats of all species, Otters, Beavers, Bears, Muskrats, and Raccoons. These scents are made of different substances. The musk of the Muskrat, contained in two glands situated just below the skin upon the back part of the abdomen, will decoy Muskrats and Minks, and perhaps Wildcats. This musk may be procured from the male in early spring. After the two glands spoken of are removed, they may be cut open, when the musk — which is a milky fluid — will appear, and may be squeezed out, mixed with alcohol, and kept for use. This musk is used in the following manner: Cut a stick of pine about six inches long, make a small cavity in one end; into this drop a little of the musk, fasten the stick in such a position that the animal to be decoyed must place his foot upon the trap in order to reach it.

Foxes, I have been informed by old trappers, are readily decoyed by using the fetid scent of the Skunk in the same manner. This scent is a greenish fluid, and is contained in glands situated in the anal region; it may be obtained in the same manner as the musk, although the operation is not pleasant. All of the above-named animals may be successfully decoyed by using an excessively fetid scent prepared during warm weather in the following manner: Take a good-sized eel or trout, and cut it in small pieces; place it in a quart bottle, cover the top with gauze to keep the flies out, hang the bottle on the south side of a fence or building, and let it remain two or three weeks, when the whole mass will become decom posed; then on the top will be found a thin layer of a clear liquid having an ineffably disagreeable odor. This fluid should be poured off carefully into a small phial and closely corked; it is to be used in the same manner as the other scents.*

Bats may be shot, or taken during daylight beneath the shingles of buildings, or in hollow trees. One or two species, however, remain outside, suspended to a branch or leaf of a tree.

Plaster may be used to absorb the flow of blood from mammals, as well as from birds.

SECTION II. *Measuring.* — To measure a mammal preparatory to skinning: Place it upon its back, then with the dividers measure the distance from the tip of the nose to the front side of the eye, record this as "the distance from the tip of the nose to the eye," then from the tip of the nose to the ear; this is "the distance from the nose to the ear"; then from the tip of the nose to the occiput, or back of the head, for "the distance from the nose to the occiput." With the rule find the distance from "the nose to the root of the tail," also the distance from "the tip of the nose to the tip of the longest toe of the outstretched hind leg"; then with the dividers find the length of the vertebra of the tail from the root; this is "the length of the tail to the end of the vertebra." With the dividers, measure the hair on the end of the tail for "the length of the hair." Measure the length of the hind leg from the knee-joint to the tip of the longest claw of the longest toe for "the length of the hind leg." Measure the length of the front leg from the elbow-joint to the tip of the longest claw of the longest toe; this is "the length of the front leg." The width of the hand is found by measuring the width of the outspread forefoot or

* This receipt was kindly given to me by Mr. George Smith of Waltham, who has used it successfully, as I have personally witnessed.

hand. Now measure the length of the ear on the back side, from the skull to the tip, for "the length of the ear." Measure "the width of the muzzle" between the two nostrils. In animals larger than a gray squirrel, measure the "girth" with a tape-measure, or piece of string, just back of the forelegs.

These measurements will answer for all excepting the bats, in measuring which proceed as before ; but, instead of the forelegs, find "the length of one wing," "the length of the wing to the hook, or thumb," and "the stretch of wings " as in birds.

Seals also vary slightly ; instead of the word " leg" use " flipper," and find the width of the hind flipper as well as the width of the fore one ; also, in addition, "the distance between the fore-flippers." The sex of a mammal is easily determined without dissecting. These measurements are to be first recorded upon a strip of paper, as in the birds, and afterwards copied into a book, as seen on the next page.

Skinning. — To skin a mammal, place it upon its back ; make a longitudinal incision in the skin over the abdomen, extending from the root of the tail about one fourth of the length of the body. Peel down each side, as in skinning a bird, pushing forward the leg so as to expose the knee-joint: sever the leg from the body at this place, and clean the bone ; proceed in this manner with the other leg. In small animals, sever the tail as close to the body as possible, leaving the bone in ; but in large animals it can generally be removed by placing two pieces of wood on each side of the bone against the skin, holding them firmly in place with one hand, and after giving a strong pull with the other the tail will slip out easily. With some animals, such as the Beaver, Muskrat, Skunk, etc., this cannot be done ; then the skin of the tail has to be opened the whole length, and the bone removed. Proceed to draw the skin

Arctomys monax.

Locality.	Age.	Sex.	Date.	No.	Nose to Eye.	Ear.	Occiput.	Root of Tail.	Outstretched Hind Leg.	Tail to End of Vertebra.	End of Hair.	Hind Leg.	Hand. Length.	Width.	Height of Ear.	Muzzle.	Girth.	Skull.* Length.	Width.	Remarks.
Ipswich	Adult	♂	1893. Aug. 22	68	1.60	2.96	2.30	13.00	15.00	4.98	6.00	3.10	2.10	.78	.85	.20	—	—	—	Light colored.
"	"	♀	" 20	55	1.57	2.80	3.45	15.50	20 15	4.50	6.75	2.80	1.85	.92	.75	—	14.50	—	—	" "
"	"	♀	" 13	43	1.32	2.94	3.45	16.25	19.50	5.45	7.60	2.85	2.05	.70	.65	.15	9.75	—	—	Top of head black.

* This measurement is taken after the animal is skinned; the width of skull is measured on the widest part, the length on the longest part.

down towards the head, until the forelegs appear; sever
these at the knee-joint, and clean the bone as before. Draw
the skin over the head, cutting off the ears close to the
skull.   Use caution in cutting the skin from the eyelids
and in severing the lips from the skull, so as not to injure their outward appearance. The skull is to be detached
entirely.   Cover the inside of the skin well with arsenic,
and, if large, rub it in well with the hand; but be sure
that every part is poisoned.

If there is any blood upon the hair, after the skin is
turned into its former position, if it is dry, remove it with
the stiff brush; if wet or *very* bloody, wash and dry with
plaster, as explained in birds.

Wind the leg-bones with sufficient hemp or cotton to
supply the place of the muscles; then fill out the head,
neck, and the rest of the body to their natural size.   Sew
up the orifice through which the body was removed neatly
over and over, drawing the edges of the skin together
nicely.

Label the skin by sewing a bit of card-board upon one
of the feet, or, if the animal is large, upon the ear, with
the number of the specimen and the sex marked upon it.
Clean the skull as much as possible with the scalpel; if
it is a large animal, the brains may be removed through
the orifice where the spinal cord enters the skull.   If this
opening is not large enough to remove them, they should
be left in.   Roll the skull in arsenic, then label it with a
number corresponding to the one upon the skin, and lay
it by for future cleaning.   The arsenic prevents insects
from attacking it.

Place the skin, if a small one, upon its side, with the
legs bent neatly; if a large one, upon its breast, with the
legs stretched out on each side, the forelegs pointing forward, the hind ones backward.   This is what is technically
called a "mammal's skin."

Very large animals, such as Deer or Bears, should not be filled out in this way, but placed flat. In skinning large animals, make an incision in the form of a double cross, by making a longitudinal cut between the hind legs, from the root of the tail to the breast, between the forelegs; then a transverse cut from the knee of the foreleg down the inside of the leg to the opposite knee. The same operation is repeated upon the hind legs. Then proceed as before, only, when the skin has been removed from the flanks, the animal must be suspended to facilitate the removal of the rest.

In skinning a mammal with horns, make a longitudinal incision from the back of the neck to the occiput, or back of the head; then make a transverse cut across the head, commencing about four inches beyond the right horn, and ending about four inches to the left of the left horn, the cut passing close to the base of the horns, thus forming a T. Remove the skin from the body as far as the neck, which is cut at its junction with the body. The skull, horns, and neck are drawn through the above-mentioned orifice.

In skinning large animals, it is well to take the diameter of the eye before it is removed, so that an artificial one may be inserted of the same size, if the animal is to be mounted, as the eyelids shrink very much while drying. All mammals should be skinned as soon as possible after they are killed, especially small ones, as in a few hours decomposition will commence; then the hair will come out.

While skinning the legs of ruminants, such as Deer, Sheep, etc., it will be found that the skin cannot be drawn over the knee-joint; then cut longitudinally through the skin below the knee, and after severing the bone at the hoof and knee, remove it through this incision. The incision should be about one fourth the length of the distance from the knee to the hoof.

Bats are to be skinned in the ordinary manner, removing the skin even to the tip of the phalanges of the wings; then tie the wing-bones together, as explained in birds. Place the bat upon a flat board to dry, and pin its wings in the proper position for flight. When dry, stitch it upon a piece of card-board.

While skinning mammals, it is sometimes necessary to use plaster to absorb the blood and other juices that are apt to flow; but if care is taken not to cut the inner skin over the abdomen it will not be needed. It is also sometimes necessary to plug the mouth and nostrils, especially if blood flows from them.

SECTION III. *Mounting Mammals.* — The art of mounting mammals in lifelike attitudes can only be acquired by experience. Hence the learner must practise the utmost degree of patience and perseverance. As in the first chapter I earnestly advised those who would be perfect to study nature, I would here repeat that advice. And if necessary while endeavoring to mount a bird, where the feathers cover the minor defects, it is essentially much more of a necessity to study nature carefully while striving to imitate the graceful attitudes and delicately formed limbs of the smaller species of mammalia, or the full rounded muscles and imposing attitudes of the larger ones; for in mammals the thin coat of hair will tend rather to expose than hide the most minute imperfections.

Perfectly stuffed specimens can only be obtained by careful measurements of all the parts, such as the size of the legs, body, etc.

In skinning mammals to mount, it is best not to remove the skull. Open it on the occipital bone, so as to remove the brains; clean well; cover with arsenic; then supply the muscles removed, by using hemp wound tightly on with thread. As the skin will shrink badly if it is stuffed loosely, carefully fill out the space occupied by the muscles of the legs in the same manner. Cut wires for the

feet, head, and tail, sharpen them on one end as directed
in mounting birds; now roll up grass until it is not quite
as large round as the body, and about one third as long.
Fill the fore part of the skin with bran or cut hemp as far
back as the shoulders, and place the ball of grass against
this filling, inside the skin. Now force the wires through
the soles of the feet and top of the head into this ball;
clinch them firmly. After filling the skin of the tail with
bran, force the wire through the grass ball to the very end;
then clinch the opposite end in the ball by cutting off the
part that protrudes and turning it in.

Fill the remaining parts of the skin with bran to the
natural size, and sew up the orifice carefully; place the
animal in the proper position by passing the protruding
wires of the feet through holes in a board, clinching them
firmly on the under side. The skin may now be moulded
into shape with the hands, the hair carefully smoothed,
the eyes set in the head with putty, the protruding wires
cut off, and the specimen set away to dry. There are
but few rules to be followed in placing animals in position, because they are almost infinite in variety. The most
imperative rule applies to the positions of the legs, which
are almost always the same; and it should be studied with
particular care, as a slight deviation from it will impair
the lifelike attitude of the specimen. The rule is: Never
place the bones of the first joint (Plate IX. No. 1) and
those of the second joint (2) of the hind legs in a *straight
line*, but always at an *angle*, more or less; while the two
bones of the forelegs (3, 4) should almost always be placed
in a straight line, — *always* when the animal is standing
upon them.

In imitating that peculiarly graceful attitude assumed
by the squirrels while sitting upon their hind legs feeding,
after imitating the curve of the back, — which not one in
a hundred can do naturally, — place the joints of the hind

legs so far up, and at such an acute angle, and the joints
of the forelegs down at such an angle, that the two will
almost touch. This rule should always be followed.

The preceding method may be applied when mounting
all animals below the size of a Newfoundland dog. Larger
animals are mounted in the following manner: Fill out
the space occupied by the muscles o. the head and legs
in the manner already described. Procure five iron rods,
with a shoulder cut at each end, upon which fit a cap
(Plate IX. Fig. 2, B); on the extreme end have a thread
cut with a nut to fit (A), — the distance between the nut
and cap should be about an inch and a half. Cut a piece
of plank, an inch and a half thick, about two thirds as
long and wide as the body of the mammal to be mounted;
bore five holes in it, as indicated in Fig. 1, A. Fasten
one rod (8) firmly to the skull by drilling a hole through
the top and placing the cap in the proper position. Screw
the nut on well (14), and place the lower end of the rod in
the hole in the plank prepared for it (11); fasten it firmly.
Now stuff the neck out with hemp to the proper size. Drill
a hole through the hoofs, or bottom of the feet, into the
hollow of the bones (2, 4); force the rod (7, 7, 7, 7) up
through this hole, through the stuffing of the legs, and
fasten them into the plank (5, 6). Force a wire into the
tail and clinch it firmly in the wood (15). By winding up
grass or hemp, imitate the various sections of the body
taken out, and place them in the proper positions (16),
making allowance for the plank and rods. Or a better
way is to take casts in plaster of the different parts and
place them in the proper position.

Everything must be solid, to avoid sinkings and depressions in the skin. In this way the student can mount
an animal of any size by increasing the size of the rods and
plank. The ends of the rods must be fastened into a
plank stand (10) by passing them through holes drilled
in it (17, 17, 17, 17).

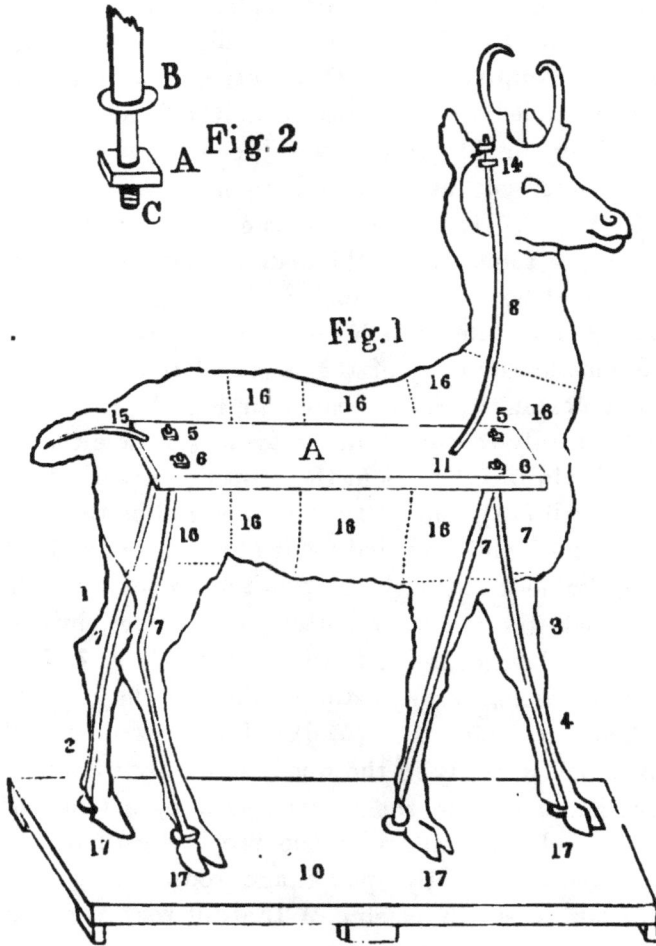

Plate IX.

To mount a dried skin, first soak it in alum-water until it is perfectly pliable, and then mount as before. The water should not be too strongly impregnated with alum, or it will crystallize upon the hair. About a quarter of a pound of alum to a gallon of water are the proper proportions. If the skull has been detached, replace it, or make an artificial one of grass or plaster to take its place. Mammals that have been preserved in alcohol may be skinned in the usual manner and mounted.

To skin mammals for the fur alone, cut in a straight line from the inside of the knee of one hind leg to the other. Skin as before explained, only cut off the feet and detach the skull. Stretch smoothly on a thin board, with the wrong side out. The skin should be lengthened rather than widened.

CHAPTER III.

THIS interesting class of animals has for a long time engaged the attention of students, yet it is surprising how comparatively little has been written about those of America. The almost infinite number of species still affords the young naturalist a wide field for careful investigation.

In collecting insects, the instruments used are : An insect-net, made of fine muslin or of silk gauze, and stretched upon a light steel wire frame, with a light handle, about four feet long, attached ; several wide-mouthed bottles and phials filled with strong alcohol ; insect-pins of the best quality, which can be procured at natural-history stores ; tweezers smaller than those used for birds (Plate I. Fig. 3) ; also, a small pair of pliers (Fig. 1) ; several soft-pine boards about twelve by twenty-four inches, planed perfectly smooth, will also be needed.

Boxes or drawers are necessary for the reception of the dried specimens, lined with thick felting or cork to receive the point of the pin that holds the insect and keeps it upright. An excellent box lined with paper is sometimes used to advantage, a description of which may be found in the "American Naturalist," Vol. I. p. 156.

I hardly need state that a good microscope is indispensable in prosecuting the study of insects, although it may be commenced without one. I shall take each order of insects separately, and endeavor to explain how they are collected and preserved, commencing with the

Beetles, or Coleoptera. — The best way to preserve beetles temporarily is by putting them instantly into strong alcohol; and as the collector will meet with specimens everywhere, he should never be without a phial ready for instant use. During spring and early summer thousands of minute species may be captured in the air with the net, especially just at night. During summer and autumn a great many nocturnal species may be captured near a light placed at an open window, or in the open air. Various species may be found feeding upon plants during the summer and autumn. A great many of the so-called carrion-beetles may be taken, during the same seasons, by exposing the carcass of an animal. Some species inhabit decayed wood, where diligent search should be made for them, especially in the woods, under old stumps or in them. Numbers of very beautiful beetles may be found in the excrements of animals, and under them, also under stones and logs of wood; they are found beneath the bark of trees and on sandy places, or in dusty roads. There are also a few aquatic species to be found in the water or near it.

To mount large beetles, force the pin through the right wing-covert near the thorax, and place the point in the cork, with the beetle's feet resting on it; place the feet in the attitude of life, with the antennæ in the proper position, with a pin on each side of them to keep them in place until dry. If the wings are to be extended, place the beetle on the pin as described; then, with an awl, bore a hole in the pine board; lay the insect upon its back, with the head of the pin in the hole; now open the wing-coverts, and spread the wings; over the latter lay a piece of card-board, and fasten it by placing pins through it into the wood on each side. The wing-coverts should not be fastened with a card, as it will flatten them. When dry, remove the card, and the wings will retain their position, when the beetle can be put in the proper position in the insect-box.

Smaller beetles, less than an eighth of an inch long,

should be fastened to a piece of mica or to a round bit of card-board with a little gum-arabic, and the pin placed through the mica or card, or they may be transfixed with very fine silver wire; this wire must then be inserted in a bit of cork, through which the common insect-pin is placed.

Beetles that are collected in remote countries should always be transported in alcohol. When they are to remain long in alcohol it should be changed once, then they will keep for years uninjured. After they have been in alcohol for two or three weeks there is no need of its covering them, as a little in the bottom of the bottle will keep them sufficiently moist; but they should never be allowed to dry.

Beetles may be preserved in a weak solution of carbolic acid as readily as in alcohol. This has the additional advantage of preserving the specimens that have been immersed in it from the ravages of noxious insects for some time. Glycerine can be used to advantage in preserving beetles that have delicate colors which fade in alcohol; but they cannot be pinned without cleansing.

Bugs, or *Hemiptera*, may be found generally upon plants. The common thistle (*Cirsium lanceolatum*) furnishes a pasture for several species. Numerous representatives of this order may be found on low bushes, and in the grass during summer and autumn. At least one species may be found in cheap boarding-houses during the midnight hours. The almost endless variety of Plant Lice come under this head, and may be taken everywhere on plants during summer and autumn.

These insects, like the beetle, are first immersed in alcohol, and afterwards placed upon pins, with the legs arranged in natural positions, and the peculiar sucking-tube, with which they are all provided, brought well forward so as to be more easily examined. The numerous

3*

aquatic species may be secured with a net ; they should
be carefully handled, however, to avoid the sharp sting, or
piercer, with which some of them are armed.

Grasshoppers, Crickets, etc., or Orthoptera. — Members of
this order may be found everywhere, — the grasshoppers in
the open fields and woods, where they may be caught in
nets.   The best way to kill them is to prick them on the
under side of the thorax with the point of a quill that
has been dipped in a solution of oxalic acid.   If they
are not to be mounted instantly, wrap them in paper.
Crickets may be found in the ground in holes or burrows,
under stones, and in the grass ; a few species may be taken
on the leaves of trees or bushes ; some species of the well-
known Cockroach may be found in houses, and some under
stones and beneath the bark of trees.

All of the above may be mounted by placing the pin
through the thorax, and arranging the legs as before described.   The wings are also extended in the same manner as the beetles', with the exception of the wing-coverts,
which are fastened with cards like the wings.

Walking-Sticks are found on low bushes or on trees, sometimes upon the ground.   They are to be put into alcohol
to kill them, then mounted like the beetles.   These insects, when dry, require delicate manipulation while being
moved, as they are *very* fragile.   When the colors of the
Orthoptera are to be preserved perfectly, place them in
pure glycerine.   This is especially necessary in preserving
the larvæ of grasshoppers.   Grasshoppers may be put into
alcohol if convenient, but it must be very strong.   This
method will generally change the colors completely.   Cock-
roaches and crickets should always be killed by placing
them in strong alcohol.

Moths and Butterflies, or Lepidoptera. — All butterflies
are diurnal, and are generally caught with the net.   They
may be killed by pinching the body just below the wings,

or by pricking between the forelegs with the quill and oxalic acid used in killing grasshoppers. If they are not to be mounted instantly, they should be packed in pieces of paper doubled in a triangular shape, with the edges folded. Butterflies may be reared from the egg by capturing the impregnated female and confining her in a box pierced with holes to allow fresh air to enter. In this box she will deposit her eggs ; these are allowed to hatch, and the larvæ fed upon the leaves that they naturally subsist upon. When sufficient time has expired they will cease to feed, and form a pupa or chrysalis, and either in a few weeks or the ensuing year come forth perfect insects, when they should be instantly killed. In this manner the collector will be able to secure fine specimens.

Although some few of the moths are diurnal in their habits, the greater part are strictly nocturnal. A great many specimens may be decoyed by the use of a bright light. During the months of May, June, July, August, and September, the following method may be practised with advantage in securing many specimens. Mix coarse brown sugar with alcohol enough to form a thick paste, saturate rags thoroughly with this paste, and hang them on trees or stakes in an open grove or wood at twilight ; or daub some of the mixture upon the stakes or trees. This mixture, thus exposed, will attract the moths. The places should be visited every few minutes with a dark lantern, taking care not to throw the light upon the spot until near enough to catch the moths in the net if they should attempt to escape.

Mr. F. G. Sanborn — who informs me that he uses the strong-smelling New England molasses in the above-described manner with success — rightly remarks "that moths may be divided into three classes by certain species of them being affected differently by the appearance of artificial light in the night. One class are powerfully *attracted* by it; another class go about their usual avocations *un-mindful* of it; while a third class are instantly *expelled* by it." The third class are by far the most difficult to capture.

Moths are easily reared from the eggs. In autumn and winter numerous cocoons may be found upon trees and bushes; these, if kept in a warm room, will hatch in early spring.

In mounting butterflies and moths I have practised the same method as described in mounting beetles, and think it superior to all others. In mounting these insects, however, it is well to use what is called a "setting-needle," to avoid rubbing the scales off the wings with the fingers.

The "setting-needle" is simply a common needle fastened into a light stick; two of these will be found useful, — one to hold the body of the insect firm, and the other to place the wings and antennæ in the proper position. The eggs and larvæ of the *Lepidoptera* should be placed in alcohol.

There is a class of moths called Hawk-Moths, Sphinxes, or Humming-Bees, some species of which are diurnal, and some nocturnal. They are all difficult to capture uninjured, as they fly rapidly, and, when caught in the net, struggle fiercely.

The larvæ, when about to form the pupa, go into the ground; for this reason the box that contains those that are being reared should be partly filled with moist earth. They are mounted in the same manner as the other *Lepidoptera*. All bright-colored insects when in the cabinet should be kept from the light as much as possible, especially those belonging to the above order.

Dragon-flies, etc., or Neuroptera. — Dragon-flies are, on account of their quick motions, somewhat difficult to capture; they are found flying over the fields and meadows; most abundant, however, in the immediate vicinity of bodies of fresh water. The lace-winged flies are also found in the vicinity of water. The larvæ of almost all of these insects are aquatic. They emerge from the water perfect insects. The larvæ should be preserved in alcohol. The perfect insects are killed with oxalic acid, and for transportation are packed in paper like the butterflies. When they are to be mounted, a copper wire is placed through the body and head; the wings are then spread, as before described.

Bees, Wasps, etc., or Hymenoptera. — Members of this order may be found everywhere in the fields and woods. Their larvæ generally resemble grubs, or maggots, and should be preserved in alcohol or glycerine.

The larvæ of the Ichneumon-Fly are found in the bodies of caterpillars. The larvæ of other species are found in the excrescences on various plants and trees. This class of insects may be caught in a net and placed in alcohol, or killed with oxalic acid. They are to be mounted as the other winged insects; the tongue must be brought forward so that it can be examined when the insect is dry.

The nests of the Wood-boring Bees, the Paper-making Wasps, and Hornets, the mud nests of the Mason Wasps, the excrescences on trees and plants, should all be collected and preserved dry after the larvæ has been taken out. Ants with their eggs and larvæ may be put into alcohol; it is best to capture these fierce little insects with the tweezers, to avoid their stings, which are sometimes poisonous.

Flies, Mosquitoes, etc., or Diptera. — These are the most difficult of all insects to preserve, especially when they have to be transported from a distance, as they must all be instantly pinned, with the exception of the Fleas, which may be put into alcohol.

They may be caught everywhere by beating bushes by the side of the roads and woods, then using the net.

Some of the species are nocturnal (as those who have slept in the open air in the woods during the warm months can bear painful testimony), and may be attracted by artificial light, as in the case of the moths, etc.   Their larvæ are found in various situations, some being aquatic, others feeding upon putrid flesh and fish ; they may be preserved in alcohol.

In closing this chapter, I would impress upon the student the absolute necessity of labelling every specimen carefully, with the date and the locality in which it is found ; this may be done by numbers referring to a catalogue, as in birds and mammals, or upon a slip of paper.   Also take notes of various circumstances relative to the habits observed at the time of capture, etc.

The best substance to protect cabinet specimens from the attacks of injurious insects is benzine, placed in an open vessel in each drawer or box. Camphor is also good, but I think that its fumes tend to fade the brighter colors of moths and butterflies.   Spirits of turpentine is good, but it evaporates much quicker than benzine.   Carbolic acid is, next to benzine, perhaps the best substance, if exposed in the same manner.

To mount insects that have been dried, place them in a box containing wet sand, and let them remain until soft, when they are mounted as before directed.   I am informed by Mr. F. G. Sanborn that a few drops of carbolic acid mixed with the water used in moistening the sand will prevent mould from forming upon them while they are being softened.   The same preventive might be put in the water used in moistening the cotton for softening bird-skins.

CHAPTER IV.

COLLECTING AND PRESERVING FISHES AND REPTILES.

SECTION I. *Fishes.* — Very many are they who at the present day follow in the footsteps of the "Father of all Anglers," the good Izaak Walton, concerning the mere *sport* of angling; but, alas! there are few who, like him, look with contemplative minds upon the great works of Nature; for the worthy Izaak was quite a naturalist, after his fashion, and loved exceedingly to prate, in his quaint style, of the wondrous birds, beasts, and fishes of which he had seen or heard. Few, indeed, are they who, although some of their happiest moments are spent by the side of the clear mountain brook, with rod in hand, see in the beautiful trout, that they with exultation draw from its sparkling home, anything more than a good dinner on the morrow.

Yet there are a few earnest naturalists who love to study the finny tribes as they ought to be studied. Indeed, the science of Ichthyology can claim among its most earnest students the greatest naturalist in our land. Those who live inland do not possess the advantages of making as extensive a collection of fishes as those who reside upon the sea-shore; nevertheless, they can all do something for this branch of natural history.

In collecting fishes the instruments generally used are nets and hooks and lines; with these try and secure every variety that can be found. Many species can be secured from the markets, where fishes are exposed for sale, by picking out the specimens that are needed. The best way to preserve fishes is to put them into alcohol. All large fishes should also be injected with alcohol before putting them in it.

There is, however, another method by which fishes may be preserved; that is, by skinning and stuffing. Thus: Open the fish on the under side from the throat nearly to the end of the body, or within a short distance of the root of the tail; then skin down each way, taking care not to scrape off any of the pigment that covers the inside of the skin and gives the fish its color; cut off the fins close to the skin on the inside, also the head at the gills; clean out the brains by enlarging the hole in the occiput, where the spinal cord enters the skull; remove the eye from the outside, dust arsenic into the orifice left, and fill it with cotto ; cover the inside of the skin with arsenic; fill it to the natural size with cotton, and sew it up; place a wire transversely through the fins to keep them in position.

. Another method is to remove the skin from one side, and to clean the flesh out in this way; the fish is then stuffed and placed upon its side, so that the opening will not show. This method will answer very well for flat fishes, but large ones must always be stuffed in the manner first described.

SECTION II. *Reptiles.* — Many a harmless snake or t ad has been sacrificed to ignorance and superstition. Indeed, so strong is the general prejudice against the most common snakes, — which are as incapable of inflicting an injury as a mouse, — that but few persons will hesitate to kill the supposed venomous reptile at sight, if indeed they have the courage to remain long enough in its vicinity to do so valiant a deed. Such persons really believe that they are removing a dangerous adversary of man from the face of the earth. I would, however, advise them to glance for a single instant at the history of these interesting — although, I will allow, somewhat disgusting-looking — animals before they again shed innocent blood. All the snakes in Massachusetts may be handled with impunity, with the exception of two species, which are very rare. I refer to the Copperhead and Rattlesnake. The prettily marked Milk Snake, or Checkered Adder, and the imaginary terrible Water Snake, are quite harmless, although we are everywhere informed by those who are ignorant upon this subject that they are exceedingly venomous. So long as people are erroneously educated in this belief, so long will the poor snakes suffer unjustly. Snakes, with but few exceptions, are neutral regarding the interest of man.

The best method of preserving snakes is to put them into alcohol moderately strong, as otherwise the scales start easily. Snakes may be benumbed by thrusting a pin into their brains; in this way they may be carried from place to place more readily than if they were uninjured.

Snakes may be skinned after making a longitudinal incision, about two inches long, in the largest part of the body, on the belly; then by drawing back the skin, the body may be divided, and the parts drawn out each way. The head should not be skinned. The eyes are removed, as in the fishes, from the outside. The skin is now covered with arsenic and turned back. It is then filled with bran to the natural size. It may, after sewing up the incision, be placed in any position desired. Artificial eyes are fixed in the head.

If the head is to be raised, run a sharpened wire through the top of it, and through that section of the neck and body that is to be elevated, through the skin into a board, cut off the protruding end, and close the skin of the head over it. After the skin becomes dry, the wire can be taken out of the board, and cut off close to the body.

Turtles may be preserved in alcohol, or they may be skinned and mounted thus: With a small steel saw cut out a square section on the under shell; remove this and draw the intestines, bones, and flesh of the legs, etc., out

E

,of the hole thus formed ; skin the legs down to the toe-
nails, removing everything ; skin the head and neck ; cover
the inside of the shell and skin with arsenic. Turn the
feet and neck back, and stuff them to the natural size
.with cotton. Fill the neck with bran ;· roll up a small ball
of grass, place it inside of the shell; then force a piece
of wire through it into the head, and clinch the end in
the ball. Pack cotton or hemp around the grass in the shell,
to keep it firm, and to fill up the empty space ; then replace the piece of shell taken out, and fasten it with glue
,or putty.

Now put the animal in the proper attitude upon a piece
.of board, and arrange the feet in the natural position, and
pin them until dry ; place the head naturally. The eyes
should be removed from the outside, and artificial ones
substituted. If it is not convenient to skin a turtle, place
it in boiling water a few moments, when the softer parts
can easily be removed from the shell. In this case, however, the bones and skull should be cleaned, labelled, and
preserved with the shell.

For scientific specimens, toads and frogs must be preserved in alcohol. But they may be skinned in the follow-
,ing manner : Open the mouth as wide as possible, and cut
.through the bone of the neck or back from the inside ; do
not cut the skin ; then separate the flesh on the inside
all around. Take hold with the thumb and forefinger, or
,with a pair of pliers, of the backbone, and press the skin
downwards, and draw the body out. When the forelegs
appear, cut the bone and flesh off to the toe-nails, and proceed to perform the same operation with the hind legs.
Cover the skin with arsenic, and turn it back, — the legs
,may be easily turned by blowing into them with the
breath. Fill the body with bran, and support the head
in a natural position with cotton until dry. Remove the
eyes from the outside, and supply their place with artificial

ones, but be sure to place them in the proper position. To place a frog or toad in a fancy attitude, place a ball of grass in the body, and wire the legs as described in small mammals.

The best time to collect toads. and frogs is during the breeding-season in spring. The salamanders may be found under stones and logs in damp places ; also some species in springs and clear running brooks, under stones. They must be placed in alcohol at once.

Lizards and alligators may be skinned in the following manner : Make an incision the whole length of the belly, and skin as described in mammals, leaving the skull in. Do not try to remove the skin from the top of the head, as it will be likely to tear. The leg-bones should be cleaned and left in. The reptile is then mounted in the same manner as a mammal. Lizards and small alligators may be put in alcohol.

The eggs of frogs and of salamanders may be preserved in alcohol. The eggs of lizards, alligators, and turtles may be blown in the same manner as birds' eggs ; but it is well to place some in alcohol if they are in an advanced state of incubation, as they will serve to illustrate the growth of the embryo. But the egg must be broken slightly to admit the alcohol to the embryo.

Last winter I accidentally made a discovery relative to the preservation of fish and reptiles. While travelling in Florida, I accidentally lost some alcohol. Being unable to replace it, and having some reptiles to preserve, I put about an ounce of carbolic acid into a glass jar, with half a pound of arsenic ; to this I added a quart of water, — I will here remark that the waters of Florida are strongly impregnated with lime. Into this composition I put some reptiles and a few young mammals. After two weeks, the jar was packed with others in a box, and sent North by express.

Upon arriving home, and opening the box, I found that the jar had become broken, and the liquid had escaped. The smaller reptiles, etc. I placed in alcohol; but a reptile known as the "Glass Snake" and a young Rabbit were left out for want of room, set away and forgotten. Upon looking them up about a month afterwards, I found, to my surprise, that the "snake" *had dried completely without shrinking in the least*, and, moreover, it *retained all the peculiar glossiness of life!* The Rabbit had not shrunk any more than if it had been in strong alcohol.

Such is the result of an accident. Whether this discovery will prove of general practical use in preserving reptiles is yet to be proven.

CHAPTER V.

SECTION I. *Crustacea.* — But few of these interesting objects of natural history live away from the salt water. The Crawfishes and a few others form the exceptions to the rule. All Lobsters, Crabs, Shrimps, and Crawfishes may be preserved dry. Wash them in fresh water, and, if the specimen is large, remove the flesh as much as possible by lifting the shield, or upper part of the shell. The specimens should be placed in as natural an attitude as possible to dry. When dry they should be handled with care, as they break easily. If arsenic is put into the body, it will help to preserve it and keep away noxious insects.

Small Crabs, Shrimps, etc. should be injected with carbolic acid and dried carefully. Never place a specimen in the sun to dry, but always in a draught of air in the shade. A great many kinds of Shrimps or Sand-Fleas may be collected from under sea-weeds on sandy beaches.

Collecting Mollusks. — Many shells may be collected on the sea-shore among the rocks at low tide. Some of the more minute species may be found clinging to the sea-weed that grows on the rocks. These require delicate manipulation, as they are very fragile; they are best removed with the tweezers, and should be placed in wide-mouthed bottles containing alcohol. Some species of cone-shaped, univalve shells may be found clinging closely to the rocks. They should be seized suddenly with the hand, and, before the animal has time to contract itself, — which it will do very quickly, and then it adheres so closely as

to render its separation from the rock without injuring
the shell extremely difficult, — removed with a sliding
motion.

Many species may be found buried in the mud and sand
below high-water mark.   The exact locality where these
are hidden may be determined by searching for their
breathing-holes on the surface of the mud or sand ; then,
by carefully removing a few inches of the soil, the shell
may be detected. Numerous species may be taken in
deep water by dredging, or with a rake, such as is used in
gathering oysters, etc.

A great many shells may be procured just as they are
cast on shore from the action of the waves; these must
be washed in fresh water and dried.   The different species
of smaller fresh-water shells may be found upon rocks,
aquatic plants, and on the surface of the mud.   They
should be placed in alcohol.   The larger species — such
as the mussels — may be taken by dredging.   Numerous
shells of mussels may be found at the entrances of the
holes of the muskrats ; of these the collector may take his
choice, as many of them are in excellent condition for the
cabinet.

The land shells, or snails, may be taken from the different plants upon which they feed, or from under stones or
logs, especially in damp places.   The smaller species should
be carefully removed with tweezers, as they are very fragile,
and placed in alcohol.   ·

Preserving Shells. — It is well to preserve in alcohol
numbers of all species of shells containing the animal.   To
remove the contents from shells that are to be dried for
the cabinet, boil them a few moments, and clean them
with a bent pin or wire.   The contents of the different
species of bivalves may be removed with a knife without
boiling, as by this method the shell retains its color much
better.   The bivalves should have their shells closed and

tied until dry. If the shells of mussels have a chalky appearance, it may be removed by immersing the specimen for a few moments in a bath of diluted muriatic acid. All shells should be carefully washed in fresh water with a tooth-brush.

Never varnish a shell; it shows bad taste to try to improve upon nature in this way, besides injuring the specimen for scientific use. As some of the more fragile land shells are liable to crack when drying, it is well to apply a slight coating of gum-arabic dissolved in water. This at some future time may be easily removed. There are also some species from which the epidermis is liable to peel; to prevent this, Mr. F. W. Putnam informs me that they should be immersed in oil for a short time.

Worms. — Marine worms may be found in the sand or mud and under stones. They should be kept in strong alcohol. Earthworms, Leeches, etc. must also be kept in alcohol.

Many species of marine worms may be found in the hulls of ships, or in wood that has been immersed in salt water for some time.

Animal Parasites. — Recently in this country, and for some time in Europe, attention has been directed by eminent naturalists to the parasites found on birds and other animals, and in their intestines. These should be placed in alcohol. The parasites from each bird or animal should be kept separate, in small phials, with the name of the bird or animal from which it was taken attached, also the date and locality.

The *Jelly-Fishes* may be found in deep water or near the shore in countless numbers. There are a great many species. They may be preserved in the following manner: After catching them in a bucket, pour off the water, and add strong alcohol, a little at a time. The animal will give out water continually during this operation, and alcohol should be added until it dies, when the water will cease flowing. It should then be removed from this solution and placed in strong alcohol, where it must be kept permanently.

Corals — which generally grow at some distance from the shore, and sometimes in deep water — should be secured with nets. They must first be washed in fresh water, then dried in the shade. It is also desirable to preserve specimens in alcohol.

Sea-Anemones are found attached to the rocks or buried in the mud; they should be plunged in strong alcohol when fully expanded, but the alcohol should afterwards be changed, as they give out large quantities of water.

Hydroids and Bryozoa. — Incrustations on the rocks, seaweeds, and delicate tufts found growing on rocks, etc., are called by these names. They may be dried or preserved in alcohol like the Corals.

Star-Fishes may be found among the rocks at low tide. They should be killed by immersing in alcohol or fresh water. Some species should be preserved in alcohol, where they should be placed in as natural attitudes as possible, as when they become rigid it is impossible to alter the position of the arms. They may be dried *in the shade* by placing them in natural positions upon a board. When dead, they should be dried instantly, as they will decompose in a few hours if kept in a damp place.

Sea-Urchins may be taken in rocky pools at low water. They may also be found under the sand on beaches, from which they are frequently washed by the waves. They may be preserved in alcohol, or dried like the Star-Fishes.

Holothurias, or *Sea-Cucumbers*, are found on flats or under stones. They must be preserved in alcohol.

Sponges and *Seaweeds* should be dried in a draught. Very pretty ornaments are made of the sea-mosses by washing them in fresh water, and spreading upon dampened paper with a fine needle; the glutinous matter contained in the plants will cause them to adhere so firmly to the paper when dried and pressed as to look like a very fine engraving or painting. When a collection of these are executed by a skilful and artistic hand, and bound in a book, they form a beautiful and interesting volume.*

SECTION 11. *Preparing Skeletons.* — I will give the methods by which bones may be cleaned. To clean the bones of large animals, first take off as much of the flesh as is possible with a knife; then put them in slatted boxes, and place the boxes in a running stream, or between tide-marks on the sea-shore. The boxes, being open, will allow the entrance of Shrimps, other aquatic animals, and insects, who will devour the meat, while the water, having free passage through, will perform its part. When well cleaned, wash them in warm soap-suds, and, after rinsing, dry in the sun and air; this will tend to bleach them.

The bones of smaller animals may also be cleansed in this manner; but the better way is either to boil them until the flesh comes off easily, or to put them into water that has been impregnated with chloride of lime; in both cases the bones will have to be cleaned afterwards with a knife and a stiff brush; they should be scraped as little as possible. If kept in a dry place, exposed to the action of the air, the bones will bleach constantly.

Mounting Skeletons. — To mount the skeleton of a bird, place a wire through the hole occupied by the spinal cord, and fasten it in the skull; this will hold the vertebra of

---

* As there is not a general interest manifested in the objects alluded to in this section, I have given but few directions for collecting and preserving them, but such as will, perhaps, satisfy the general collector. Those who are particularly interested in them will find in the pages of the various numbers of the "American Naturalist" more particular directions for collecting and preserving each branch of this truly interesting class of animals, written by the most competent and well-informed men in our country

4

the neck and tail, and other bones of the back, in position.
Next, force a wire through the hollows in the bones of the
tarsi, tibia, and hips (Plate X. k, y, j) by drilling a hole
through each end; now fasten this wire to the broad bone
that covers the back (m), by drilling a hole through on
each side and bending the wire down firmly (x), first over
then under the bone, where it meets the end of the opposite wire; twist the ends together. The wing, breast, and
other bones are now fastened on by drilling holes transversely through the ends and running wires through and
twisting them (r, d).

The skeletons of mammals, fishes, etc. are mounted in
much the same manner. If large, they are supported on
iron rods. The wire used must be composed of brass or
copper, as iron corrodes easily. The fleshy or cartilaginous
parts of the feet should be removed, but not the outer or
horny portion of the bill.

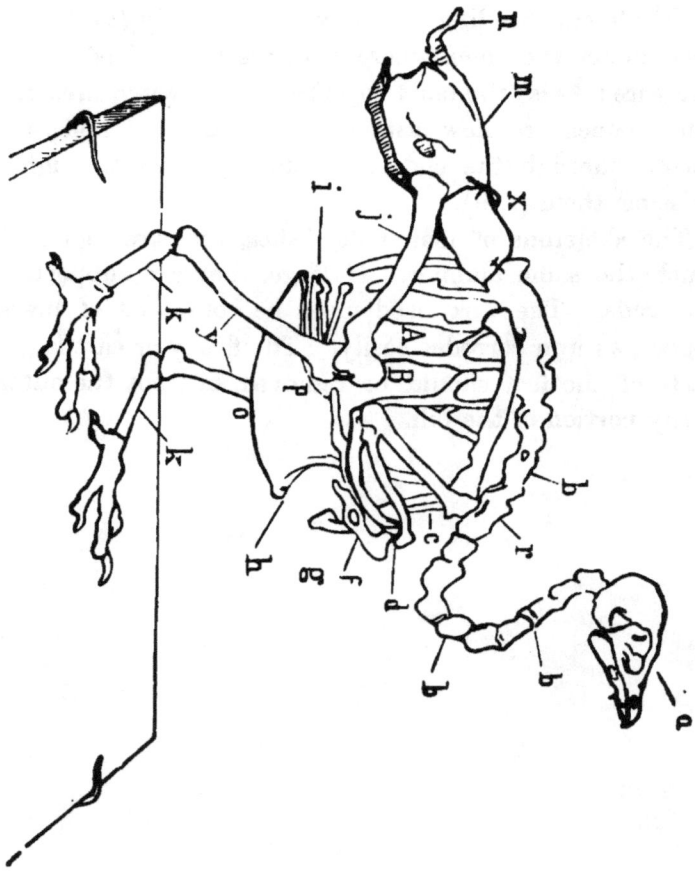

Plate X

CHAPTER VI.

COLLECTING AND PRESERVING EGGS.

No portion of natural history has received more attention than the science of Oölogy; yet in very many cases collections of eggs are made in such a careless manner as to render them worthless, except as ornaments, on account of the collector's not paying sufficient attention to *identification* and *authentication*.

Let identification, then, be the collector's first care; let him make it a rule *never* to take an egg or nest until he can surely tell to what species it belongs. The best method of learning the name of the owner of the nest is to shoot her, especially by collectors who have had but little experience in studying birds; while the more practised ornithologist can generally tell at a glance, if the bird is large, what it is. While collecting the eggs of the Warblers and other small birds, the most experienced oölogist should *never* neglect to shoot the bird, even if he has to watch for it a long time.

Nests and eggs should never be labelled on the authority of a person who has found them, and only *seen* the birds, but who is in a comparative degree unacquainted with them. The nest should be seen *in situ*, and the bird identified. I have known a great many errors to arise from this source.

Commence early in spring to look for the nests of the rapacious birds, and continue the search for these and other nests until late in summer. I know of no rule to be followed in finding nests. Search long and diligently in every locality frequented by birds; and watch them while building. Place straw, hay, cotton, hemp, or any of the materials that birds use in constructing their nests, in an exposed situation in a swamp or wood, then by watching the birds when they come to take it, and following them, many nests will be found that would otherwise escape notice.

To remove the contents of an egg, drill a small hole in one side with a drill made for this purpose (Plate I. Figs. 5, 6) ; two sizes of these drills will be required. Now, with the blow-pipe — of which two sizes are also needed, (Fig. 7) — applied to the lips, force a small stream of air into the hole ; this will cause the contents, if fresh, to escape at the *one* hole. To prevent breakage while drilling the eggs of the Humming-Birds, or other small birds, it is well to cover the outer surface with thin paper, gummed securely on, and dried.

To remove the contents of an egg that has the embryo partially developed, drill as before, only a larger hole is necessary ; then with a small hook (Fig. 8) remove the embryo in small pieces ; after which introduce water with the blow-pipe to rinse the interior of the egg. If the contents are allowed to remain in a few days, it will facilitate their removal. If the egg is covered with paper, as in the case of the Humming-Birds, the edges of the hole will be less liable to be injured by the shell being broken while using the hook.

Never make holes at the end of the egg, or on opposite sides , but if this old method is still preferred, they should both be made *on one side*, with the larger one nearest the greater end.

The best method that I know of for authenticating eggs is the following : After the egg is blown, place a number, written with ink, upon it, corresponding with one placed in the nest, then draw a line beneath it ; under this line place the number of the egg in the nest : thus $\frac{20}{4}$ would mean that the nest is No. 29, and the egg is the No. 4 of that nest; both of these numbers will refer to a book, where all the particulars of the finding of the nest, the locality, measurements of the nest, eggs, etc. in inches, are recorded.

The method of preparing a book like that referred to above may be seen in the following specimen : —

Scops asio.

No. of Eggs.		Locality.	Date.	Land.	Tree.	Situa-tion of Nest.	Height from Ground.	Diameter and Depth of Hole.	Remarks. Nest No.
Length	Width	Weston	1868. April 27	Low	Oak	Hole	30 ft.	5 in. 12 in.	29 Nest composed of leaves
1 1.50	1.27								
2 1.46	1.20								
3 1.45	1.25								
4 1.47	1.27								
5 1.50	1.25								

The measurements of an egg are taken with the dividers in hundredths of an inch.   The number is attached to the nest.   Nests, if composed of loose materials, must be kept in boxes, separated from each other ; if lined with feathers, benzine should frequently be applied, to prevent their being attacked by moths.

PART II.

—•—

CATALOGUE

OF

THE BIRDS OF EASTERN MASSACHUSETTS,

WITH

NOTES RELATIVE TO THEIR MIGRATION, HABITS,

ETC., ETC., ETC.

4*

PART II.

INTRODUCTION.

ORNITHOLOGISTS of the present day are much indebted to the earnest and enthusiastic men who studied the habits of our birds in years past; but truthful and careful though they may have been, being but *men*, they were fallible. As this is an age of advancement, it behooves us of the present day, while we are in a measure guided by these teachings, not to be biased by their conclusions, that we may detect the errors which they unconsciously committed.

If, while endeavoring to correct some deeply seated error of the past, we disagree with our brother ornithologists, let us, with the spirit of the true naturalist, who would advance the study of Natural History, bring infallible proofs of its being an error, thereby convincing without offending.

If in the following pages I unwittingly make mistakes, I am ready to be convinced by sufficient proof.

In separating birds into species, too much dependence has been placed upon exceedingly variable characters as valid specific distinctions. For instance, the bill, although in the main retaining its shape, is sometimes subject to wide differences; this is well illustrated in the Terns, where they are extremely changeable in the length and curve of the culmen; they also vary in coloration; yet in determining species, these points are now, and always have been, considered of value.

The comparative length of the quills is another very

inconstant character, and in but few cases can it be depended upon. This has been used as a distinguishing mark in separating some of the smaller Flycatchers. I have tested it, and found it to be valueless, as there is no rule relative to age or sex by which this is governed.

Again, intensity and paleness of color have been almost unanimously considered of specific value. Indeed, some species have been formed *wholly* upon this peculiarity! (Witness *Turdus Aliciæ*.) Spots and bars on the wings, and streaks on the rump, are characters changing with age and season, and should *never* be depended upon.

Another thing is the difference in size; any one who has collected, and carefully measured, birds of one species from one locality, in any numbers, will at once be convinced of the absurdity of paying any attention to this particular in determining specific characters. As pertinent, I wish here to announce a somewhat surprising discovery that I have made. After a careful measurement of over three thousand specimens, I have been convinced of the fact, *that birds for a certain period increase in size, after which they gradually decrease.* Whether the period of decrease is limited or not during the life of the bird, I am unable at present to state. The period of *increase* may also be variable, both specifically and individually, which yet remains to be proven. Both the increase and decrease are proportional; feet, bill, wings, and body alike keep equal pace. This rule is not without its exceptions, but in the majority of cases it is *the rule*, and I offer it to my fellow-laborers to prove and use in their ornithological investigations.

Besides those named, there are other distinctions used in determining species, that in some cases are inconstant. I think it advisable always, before attempting to separate a supposed species from one closely allied, to procure a sufficiently large number of specimens, and carefully study these seeming distinctions, and decide if they are constant.

Specific characters are. I believe, sufficiently tangible and constant in nature, and never need be mistaken ; this will hereafter be illustrated. I would, however, first speak strongly in disfavor of the growing belief in the hybridism of birds. I do not believe that, generally speaking, hybrids occur ; there are a few cases, but they are exceptions. In many instances the so-called hybrids are but abnormal conditions of plumage, that can be accounted for on entirely natural grounds. But sometimes the ornithologist, in his haste to make new species, has divided the two opposite stages of color in one species, calling each by a different specific name, and has afterwards found specimens that in their peculiar plumage, size, etc. naturally form connecting links between the two ; in his perplexity as to which of these to refer it, he has hit upon the fortunate (?) expedient of calling it a "hybrid." Would it not have been much better, if, at first, he had taken a large number of specimens, and, studying them, seen what the supposed hybrids really were ?

I have yet to meet with a single instance of hybridism even among local races, although these perhaps occur — but, I think, seldom — among well-defined species while undomesticated.

Species consists in a bird's having certain characters so well defined, although inconstant (but never variable beyond a certain point), that it may readily be distinguished from others. Take, for an illustration, the Robin, a bird that since its discovery has never had a single variety or local race called a "new species" (at which I marvel greatly, however). The typical specimen has a clear red breast, black head, and immaculate slate-colored back and wings, which at once distinguish it from all others of the *Turdinæ*. We also have a Robin that is very light-colored, with the red almost obsolete, the wings sometimes spotted, and the black of the head pale. Perhaps it is a much smaller bird than the average, but no one thinks of calling this a "new species"; although, if it were not for the fact that there are Robins presenting every shade in color and difference in size between this and the typical specimen, it would certainly be a good species. Why are not the same variations, which we can here see at a glance, discovered in the other members of this family? They certainly exist. But more of this anon.

The Robin has also characters that it bears in common with other *Turdinæ*, which are its true generic characters. If, then, we cannot establish a connecting link in the manner described between one species and its nearest allies, we may be sure that it never * mixes with others in breeding, but always mates with one having the same peculiarities as itself, although changeable to a certain point. This constitutes a natural species. If, on the other hand, we *do* find a connecting link, many times repeated in different individuals, between a supposed species and its nearest ally, we may be sure that they are one.

In the succeeding pages I have followed the classification of Professor W. Lilljeborg, of Upsala, as adopted provisionally by the Smithsonian Institution. The original method being the ascending or progressive mode, while the one used is the descending mode, with other minor changes.

This classification is by far the best in use, although, perhaps, not perfect. By the old methods the Vulture, vile feeder of carrion, was placed *first*, and we were told to look to him as king of the birds. But King Vulture has been dethroned, and in his stead reigns the Thrush king over all; crowned for his sprightly intelligence and

---

* The well-known exceptions to this rule are *Colaptes auratus* mixing with *C. Mexicanus;* two of the *Juncos*, and perhaps others

lively song, and he has not his equal. As before, however, the birds that approach nearest the fishes are rightfully placed the lowest (Penguins, Grebes, Divers, etc.).

In writing the present catalogue I have received much assistance from the excellent list of Dr. Eliot Coues; also from the very complete list of Mr. J. A. Allen, to whom I express my sincere thanks for other services. I am also under obligations, for valuable information, to Mr. William Brewster, of Cambridge; Professor S. F. Baird, of the Smithsonian Institution; Mr. H. B. Farley, of Chelsea; Mr. E. L. Weeks, of Newtonville; Mr. J. F. Le Baron, of Ipswich; and especially to Mr. Henry A. Purdie, of West Newton, for valuable notes concerning the time of migration, etc.

In giving the time of migration, I have taken the average for many years, or the earliest or latest date observed during a similar period.

All information that I have received has been accredited to the individuals who have given it. The occurrence of all other birds, or notes upon them, I have given upon my own authority. When facts about some particular species are well known, having been published before, I have not repeated them.

C. J. M.

NEWTONVILLE, September 20, 1869.

CATALOGUE.

TURDIDÆ, — The Thrushes.

1. **Turdus migratorius,** Linn. — *Robin.* Common summer resident; abundant everywhere; breeds as abundantly A few winter regularly; but I am inclined to think that these are visitors from the north, and do not reside during summer. The regular summer residents arrive in the latter part of February, and depart in November.

2. **Turdus nævius,** Gm. — *Varied Thrush.* Has been taken once, at Ipswich, in December. It is, however, entirely accidental.

3. **Turdus mustelinus,** Gm. — *Wood Thrush.* Moderately common summer resident; nests on low bushes or trees in swampy woods or thickets. I have found the nest, with young, as early as June 4th. The usual time of nesting in this section is, however, about June 1st. Arrives from May 11th to 18th, departs about the middle of October.

I have invariably found this bird exceedingly shy and difficult to approach. It may be seen in early morning, and during the evening twilight, in the breeding-season, perched on the topmost bough of some tall tree, pouring out a flood of delightful melody. In autumn it does not sing, and is seldom seen.

4. **Turdus Pallasii,** Cab. — *Hermit Thrush.* Very common during its migrations, especially in autumn, when

it is found everywhere in the woods. In the spring it frequents the swampy woods, and is more shy. Arrives from
the south from April 9th to 22d ; remains about two weeks,
when it departs northward. Arrives from the north about
October 1st. Becomes very plentiful by the 10th. By the
1st of November the greater part disappear, although a few
remain until quite late in the month. Have taken it in
Coos County, northern New Hampshire, on October 31st,
although the ground was covered with snow six inches deep
at the time ! also in Oxford County, Maine, as late as November 6th.

I have never heard it give any note, except a low chirp
of alarm, while passing through Massachusetts. A few
undoubtedly breed here. I have seen it at Hyannis on
July 3, 1868. There is also a nest containing four eggs,
labelled as belonging to this bird, collected at North Bev-
erly, June 14, 1868, by Mr. E. P. Emmerton, in the museum of the Peabody Academy of Science at Salem.

5. **Turdus fuscescens**, STEPH. — *Wilson's Thrush*,
Tawny Thrush, " Veery." Common summer resident. Arrives from April 30th to May 12th ; leaves about the 1st
of September. Found everywhere in the woods, where it
breeds abundantly.

6. **Turdus Swainsonii**, CAB. — *Olive-backed Thrush*.
Rather rare spring and autumn migrant. Have taken it
from May 16th to June 1st in spring, and in autumn from
September 25th until October 9th. Frequents thick, swampy
woods and thickets, where, from its shy and retiring habits,
it is very difficult to detect. This bird is quite variable in
size and intensity of color, insomuch that ornithologists have
long considered specimens of a somewhat larger size (although not always) and of a universally pale color, a "new"
and a "good species," called the "Gray-cheeked Thrush"
(*Turdus Aliciæ*, Baird). It is strange that when the wide
differences in this family are so well known and so generally

acknowledged, regarding the intensity of color and size, that ornithologists will persist in regarding them as characters of specific value. And more incomprehensible still is the fact, that well-reasoning ornithologists cannot see the often-repeated and perfectly natural connecting links, both in intensity of color and size, between the two extremes, and understand the fact of their being connecting links, but prefer rather to depart from the great and (I believe) unvarying laws that the mighty Ruler of the universe has established for the maintenance of species inseparable since their creation, and call them "hybrids."

If in our *furor* for forming new species we admit such intangible characters as these to be of specific value, we cannot consistently stop here, but out of this one species alone we must (governed by these laws) make at least six! For I have seen as many constant stages of plumage among specimens of *T. Swainsonii*, besides numerous so-called hybrids. But enough has already been written by Mr. J. A. Allen in the "Memoirs of the Boston Society of Natural History," Vol. I. Part IV., commencing on page 507, upon this subject, to convince any one who will examine for himself of the invalidity of "*Alicia*" as a species.* Mr. Allen has given the subject much thought, and presents it in the right light.

7. **Seiurus† aurocapillus**, SWAIN. — *Golden-crowned Thrush*, "Oven-Bird." A very common summer resident, found everywhere in the woods. Its curiously covered nest is placed on the ground. Arrives from May 2d to 10th; leaves about the middle of September.

* Examine "'Birds of Springfield,' Proceedings Essex Institute," Vol. IV. pp. 56–58; also " American Naturalist," Vol. II. p. 622.

† This genus which has long been placed with the *Sylvicolidæ*, I think closely allied to the true Thrushes. Its habits as well as its anatomical structure, give it a place among the *Turdidæ*. Members of this genus might properly bear the name of Terrestrial Thrushes.

8. **Seiurus noveboracensis**, NUTT. — *Water Thrush*, "Water Wagtail." Not uncommon during the migrations. Have taken it from May 15th to 27th. It passes Massachusetts in September. It is found in swampy thickets, and on the edges of streams, ponds, and pools of water. It is not very shy, and in its actions reminds one of a Sandpiper. It may possibly breed here, but I have never detected it during the summer months. It has, while with us in spring, a singularly pleasing song.

The Large-billed Water Thrush (*Seiurus Ludovicianus*, Bonap.) ought to occur, as I have seen a specimen that was taken by my friend, Mr. Allen, near Springfield.

9. **Harporhynchus rufus**, CAB. — *Brown Thrush*, "Thrasher," "Ferruginous Mocking-Bird." Common summer resident ; breeds abundantly ; nests on low bushes or on the ground, — more frequently in the latter situation. Arrives from April 23d to May 4th ; departs about the 1st of October.

10. **Mimus Carolinensis**, GRAY. — *Cat-Bird*. One of the most common and best known of all our birds ; also very beneficial to the husbandman, in spite of the almost universal prejudice against it. Breeds abundantly near houses, in hedges, along the edges of woods, or in swampy thickets. Arrives from April 29th to May 7th ; takes its departure about the middle of October.

11. **Mimus polyglottus**, BOIE. — *Mocking-Bird*. Has been taken in the western part of the State. I have never seen a specimen in this region, but Mr. N. Vickery informs me that he has seen one that was taken some years ago in Lynn.

SAXICOLIDÆ, — THE ROCK-INHABITERS.

12. **Sialia sialis**, BAIRD. *Blue-Bird*. — Common ; breeds abundantly in holes in trees or in martin-boxes.

Arrives as early as February 27th; becomes common by March 10th; leaves about the 1st of November.

SYLVIIDÆ, — THE WARBLERS.

13. **Regulus calendulus,** LICHT. — *Ruby-crowned Kinglet.* Common spring and autumn migrant. Arrives in spring, from April 10th to 22d; remains until the first week in May; arrives from the north the second, and departs south the last, week in October. Found in the woods and orchards everywhere.

14. **Regulus satrapus,** LICHT. — *Golden-crowned Kinglet.* Abundant winter resident. Found everywhere. Have taken it from October 14th until May 9th. Commonly seen in company with the Chickadee.

The Blue-gray Gnatcatcher (*Polioptila cærulea,* Sclat.) is said to occur. I have never met with it in this section.

PARIDÆ, — THE TITMICE.

15. **Parus atricapillus,** LINN.—*Black-capped Titmouse,* "Chickadee." Abundant resident. Found everywhere; no bird is better known. Builds its nest by drilling a hole in a partly decayed tree, generally a birch. It sometimes, however, occupies other holes in trees. It builds its nest about the first of May.

CERTHIIDÆ, — THE CREEPERS.

16. **Certhia familiaris,*** LINN. — *Brown Creeper.* Resident. Rather rare during summer, but common in winter. Found everywhere, — in the woods, in orchards,

* The supposed difference between the American and European *Certhia* is not tangible, therefore the specific name of *Americana* becomes a synonyme.

and on the elm-trees in the streets of the villages.   Said
to build its nest in May in holes of trees.

SITTIDÆ, — The Nuthatches.

17. **Sitta Carolinensis,** Gm. — *White-bellied Nuthatch.* Common resident, perhaps more so during spring
and autumn ; breeds.   I have seen the young fully fledged
by June 6th.

18. **Sitta Canadensis,** Linn. — *Red-bellied Nuthatch.*
Rather common winter resident.   Arrives about the middle of October.   Perhaps a few remain to breed, as I have
taken it in the latter part of May.   Found in the woods
everywhere.

TROGLODYTIDÆ, — The Wrens.

19. **Troglodytes aëdon,** Vieill. — *House Wren.*
Common summer resident, but exceedingly local in its
distribution.   In Newton it is very rare during the breeding-season, while in Cambridge it breeds abundantly.   Arrives from April 30th to May 20th ; leaves about October 1st.

After a critical examination of a large series of Wrens
I have come to the conclusion that the so-called " Wood
Wren " (*Troglodytes Americanus,* Aud.) is this species in
unusually dark plumage.   I have in my possession birds
exhibiting the well-known marks of immaturity, as generally paler colors, with spots upon the wings.   With such
birds the superciliary stripe is better defined.   But this
character is variable, and cannot be depended upon.   I
have also birds with generally darker colors, with the
superciliary stripe wanting or barely perceptible.   The
wings are unspotted, and the breast exhibits faint undu-
lating transverse lines or bars of darker.   These are the

extremes ; I have birds exhibiting every shade of color between, but remarkably variable.

Upon these inconstant characters does the specific value of *Americana* rest ! Very pertinent then are the grave doubts expressed by ornithologists as to its validity as a species. The following is an accurate description of the specific characters, with the more important synonymes, and a table of comparative measurements.

Troglodytes aëdon, VIEILL. — *House Wren.*

Troglodytes aëdon.	VIELLOT, Ois. Am. Sept. II. 1807, 32; Pl. CVII. — IB. Nouv. Dict. XXXIV. 1819, 506.
" "	BONAP., Obs. Wilson, 1825, No. 136.
" "	RICH , F. Bor. Am. II. 1831, 316.
" "	AUD., Orn. Biog. I. 1831, 427: V. 1839; Pl. LXXXIII.— IB. Syn. 1839, 75. — IB. Birds Am. II 1841, 125; Pl. VIII.
" "	BAIRD, Birds N. Am. 1858, 367.
" "	SAMUELS, Orn. and Oöl. of N. Eng. 1867, 196.
" "	COUES, Proc. Essex Inst. V. 1867, 278.
Sylvia domestica	WILSON, Am. Orn. I. 1808, 129; Pl. VIII.
Troglodytes fulvus.	NUTTALL, Man. I. 1832, 422.
" "	RICH., List, 1837.
Troglodytes Americanus.	AUD., Orn. Biog. II. 1834, 452: V. 1839, 469, Pl. 179. — IB. Birds Am. II. 1841, 123; Pl. 119. — IB. Syn. 1839, 75.
" "	BAIRD, Birds N. Am. 1858, 368.
" "	COUES, Proc. Essex Inst. V. 1867, 278.

SP. CH. — Bill extremely variable in size, dark brown, paler at the base of the lower mandible. Upper parts dark brown, becoming more rufous on the rump and upper tail-coverts ; middle of back and upper tail-coverts faintly barred transversely with irregular lines of darker. The brown of the back is exceedingly changeable; when it becomes light-colored, these bars are almost, if not quite, obsolete ; wings distinctly and more regularly barred transversely with black ; tail reddish brown, irregularly but distinctly barred transversely with black, — sometimes this black has a lighter edging ; under parts dirty white, becoming pale brown on sides, abdomen, and under tail-coverts. Middle of breast, sometimes, and sides, faintly and irregularly barred with transverse lines of pale brown. During autumn and winter this pale brown of the sides, abdomen, and under tail-coverts, becomes quite rufous, and the bars on the sides much more distinct. Abdomen and under tail-coverts more regularly and distinctly barred transversely with dark brown; eyes brown. Feet varying from brown to paler, sometimes almost white. In this stage it is the *T. Americanus* of authors.

In younger stages the plumage differs from this in having the upper parts paler, with the bars on the middle of the back almost, and in some specimens quite, obsolete. The bars on the wings are not as distinct, and there are on the ends of the wing-coverts small triangular spots of dirty white. There is generally a dirty-white superciliary stripe over the eye. The middle of the breast is without the faint barrings. The under mandible of the bill is sometimes pale brown the whole length. This is the *T. aëdon* of authors.*

The first stage is somewhat uncommon, while the intermediate and the last are of more general occurrence.

It will be seen by the table, that no rule can be fixed where color can be made to coincide with size.

20. **Anorthura hyemalis**, RENNIE. — *Winter Wren.* Rare in this section during the migrations. I have seen it in October and in April. I have never met with it in winter, and doubt if it occurs during that season. I found it very abundant in Oxford County, Maine, from October 12th to 22d, when it disappeared. Frequents low bushes by the roadside and along stone walls. It is shy, and difficult to approach while it is in sight, as upon the appearance of man it immediately hides.

21. **Cistothorus stellaris**, CAB. — *Long-billed Marsh*

---

* Occasionally the young-of-the-year assume the darker plumage of the adult : this was the case with No. 2970.

Table of Measurements of T. aëdon.

No.	Age	Sex.	Locality.	Length.	Stretch.	Wing.	Tail.	Bill.	Tar-sus.	Longest Quill.‖	Date of Collection. 1869.	Remarks.
1900	Adult *	♂	Jacksonville, Fla.	4.70	6.50	2.44	2.40	.47	.50	4th	Jan. 1	Dark colored.
1942	" *	♂	"	5.00	6.80	2.00	1.70	.50	.57	4th	Jan. 1	" "
1936	" †	♂	"	5.00	6.75	2.05	1.75	.50	.65	4th	Jan. 3	" "
1967	" †	♂	"	4.75	6.75	2.05	1.95	.52	.65	4th	Jan. 3	" "
1968	" †	♂	"	4.50	6.50	2.06	1.65	.50	.61	4th	Jan. 3	—
2033	" †	♀	"	5.70	6.75	2.10	1.75	.80	.60	4th	Jan. 17	—
2730	" •	♀	"	5.65	6.95	2.00	1.64	.51	.54	3d	March 30	Dark colored.
2576	" †	♂	Dummitt's, E Fla.	5.00	6.50	2.10	2.00	.50	.62	4th & 5th	March 10	" "
2388	Young §	♀	"	5.00	6.70	1.90	1.70	.50	.65	2d & 3d	March 11	Rather pale.
2984	Adult §	♀	Watertown, Mass	5.00	5.00	2.00	1.65	.50	.62	2d & 3d	June 9	Pale.
1979	"	♀	Jacksonville, Fla.	4.80	6.50	2.00	1.30	.46	.60	2d & 4th	Jan. 5	" "
2909	" †	♀	Cambridge, Mass.	4.50	—	1.70	1.45	.45	.55	2d & 3d	June 23	" "
2970	Young-of-year.‡	♂	Newton, Mass	5.15	7.00	2.12	2.80	.50	.67	3d	Sept. 6	Dark colored.

* Intermediate, but approximating to *Americanus.*

† In the plumage described as *Americanus.*

‡ Plumage described as the typical *aëdon.*

§ Intermediate, but approximating to *aëdon.*

‖ I give the longest quill of each bird to show the absurdity of making this a valid specific character, as was done by the old authors.

Wren. Common in the large fresh-water marshes during summer, where it breeds during the latter part of May.

22. **Cistothorus palustris,** CAB. — *Short-billed Marsh Wren.* Rather more common than the preceding. Frequents the same localities. It is exceedingly difficult to procure, on account of its lying very closely when hunted.

MOTACILLIDÆ, — THE WAGTAILS.

23. **Anthus Ludovicianus,** LICHT. — *Tit-lark.* Abundant spring and autumn migrant along the coast. I am informed by my friend, Mr. William Brewster, that it is also abundant on the Fresh Pond marshes, near Cambridge. It has the habit of jerking its tail like the Water Thrushes.

SYLVICOLIDÆ, — THE WOOD-WARBLERS.

24. **Mniotilta varia,** VIEILL. — *Black and White Creeper.* Common summer resident. Abundant during the migrations. Found in the woods everywhere. Arrives the last week in April; leaves the latter part of September. Breeds.

25. **Parula Americana,** BON. — *Blue Yellow-backed Warbler.* Summer resident. This beautiful little Warbler seems to be a somewhat irregular visitor while migrating. During the spring of 1867 it was very abundant; in 1868 I could find but two or three, although I searched diligently for it; while the season of 1869 brought it in particular abundance. Found generally in oak woods. Arrives about the second week in May; leaves in the middle of September. Mr. William Brewster informs me that it breeds quite commonly in certain localities.

26. **Geothlypis trichas,** CAB. — *Maryland Yellow-*

throated Warbler. Abundant summer resident; breeds, commonly in marshy or swampy places. Arrives from May 1st to 13th; leaves about the first week in October or the latter part of September.

27. **Geothlypis Philadelphia,** BAIRD. —*Mourning Warbler.* Very rare. May 21, 1866, Mr. William Brewster shot a male in Cambridge, on the top of a tall tree. Another specimen of the same sex was taken at the Franconia Mountains, New Hampshire, on August 3, 1867. "It was in company with four fully fledged young, which it was feeding. The young, being shy, and in a thicket of low bushes, were not procured. The old bird was catching flies after the manner of the Flycatchers." * I have met with this species but once; that was in May, among low bushes, in a swampy place.

28. **Oporornis agilis,** BAIRD. — *Connecticut Warbler.* Very rare, especially during spring. I can record but four instances of its capture, — a male, among low bushes, in Newton Centre, on September 16, 1867, by Mr. L. L. Thaxter; I procured another male in September, 1868, also among low bushes, in a swampy place. My specimen was very shy. It was exceedingly fat; I never met with a bird more so. Mr. H. A. Purdie has also taken specimens twice in September.

29. **Icteria viridis,** BON. — *Yellow-breasted Chat.* Exceedingly rare summer visitor. Shot a male in full plumage in a swampy thicket in the spring of 1862. This is the only instance recorded of its capture in this locality.

30. **Helminthophaga ruficapilla,** BAIRD. — *Nashville Warbler.* Common on the migrations. A few breed. Arrives from May 6th to 18th; departs in September. Frequents the woods everywhere, generally keeping near the tops of the trees or on the higher branches.

* MS. Notes of Mr. W. Brewster.

31. **Helminthophaga peregrina,** Cab. — *Tennessee Warbler.* Very rare spring and autumn migrant. Between the 18th and the 24th of May, 1869, I shot four specimens, all males, on apple-trees in Newtonville. This is the first record of its capture in Eastern Massachusetts. A pair, male and female, were shot by Mr. William Brewster, near Mount Auburn, on high oak-trees. It has a very pleasing note. Its breeding place is unknown; probably in the northern sections of New England, however, it finds a secure home.

32. **Helminthophaga pina,** Baird. — *Blue-winged Yellow Warbler.* Mr. E. A. Samuels gives it as a very rare summer resident. "In 1857, in the month of May, about the 12th or 15th, I found a small flock in Dedham, Massachusetts." * It is also given, by other ornithologists, as very rare. I have never met with it.

33. **Helminthophaga chrysoptera,** Baird.— *Golden-winged Warbler.* Rather common summer resident. Arrives from May 15th to 29th.

I had long suspected this beautiful Warbler of breeding with us; this season my suspicions were confirmed. The following is an extract from my note-book: —

. "*June 12, 1869.* — Walking this morning in a lane that goes through a piece of woods in West Newton, my attention was attracted by hearing the sharp alarm-note of a female of this species, who was sitting upon a small elm-tree by the roadside, within a few yards of me. Knowing by her actions that she had a nest in the immediate vicinity, I retreated a few rods and watched her. In a few moments she flew down into the grass and tall weeds at the foot of the tree. I waited a little, then went quickly to the spot; after a short search I discovered the bird sitting on the nest almost at my feet! She instantly flew off, and alighted upon a tree near by, disclosing to my

* "Ornithology and Oölogy of New England," 1867, p. 213.

delighted gaze the eggs. They were the first I had ever seen, and I was much pleased. Full well was I now repaid for all my former searching through swampy thickets and briery hedges for this bird's nest.

" *The locality* chosen was within a few feet of a lane where an occasional pedestrian passed, and within eight rods of a travelled road! These facts are surprising, inasmuch as the general habitat of this bird is in lonely, swampy places, remote from man and his ways. About twenty rods away was a swampy thicket; from this the land sloped gradually up to the spot where the nest was placed. There was, apparently, no attempt at concealment whatever; to be sure, at the time of discovery it was partly overshadowed by some ferns and rank weeds; but these must have grown after the nest was built, and it was plainly perceptible to a person standing upright. It was placed upon a small bit of green moss, without the slightest depression of the ground; indeed, the spot, if anything, was slightly elevated above the surrounding surface. Over all waved the branches of the pretty little elm upon which I first saw the bird. There were a few scattering oak and elm trees in the immediate vicinity.

" *The nest* is composed outwardly of large oak-leaves, of the previous year, and grapevine bark, and is lined, not very smoothly, with fine grass and a few horse-hairs. It is large for the size of the bird, quite deep, and slightly smaller in diameter at the top than in the middle. The whole structure is not nearly as neat as would be expected from so small and elegant a bird, and reminds one strikingly of the nest of the Maryland Yellow-throat. The dimensions are: Depth externally 3.15 inches, internally 2.20. Diameter internally in the middle 2.25, at the top 1.90; diameter externally 3.50.

" *The eggs* are four in number, very prettily marked, and proportionate to the size of the bird. No. 1 is per-

fect in form ; measures .67 × .55, and is pure white, spotted
and blotched with reddish brown, thickly at the larger and
sparsely at the smaller ends. No. 2, also perfect ; measures
.66 × .55 ; is spotted at the larger end, but not as thickly
as No. 1 ; *very* sparsely at the smaller end. No. 3, perfect ; measures .66 × .55 ; but few spots on the larger
end compared with the others ; the spots on the smaller
end are few and scarcely perceptible. No. 4 is not so perfect in form, being smaller in the middle ; measures .67 ×
.50 ; the spots on the larger end form an irregular ring
around a comparatively clear centre ; the egg is but little
spotted elsewhere. There was also a Cow-Bunting's egg in
the nest." *

It is a strange fact that among all the birds of this
species I have seen, I have never met with a female before. I will here give a short description, as compared
with the plumage of the male, of the one which I shot, as
it differs from that given by others. The yellow on the
wings is as bright as in the male, and that of the crown
nearly as bright. Not as much white on the tail. The
throat and cheeks, black in the male, are in this case slate.
The middle of the back, which, in the perfectly mature
male, — with which this should be compared, as it is evidently a perfectly mature female, — is of a beautiful pearl
gray, in this case is strongly tinged with the greenish
shade seen in young males. The under parts are yellowish instead of a clear white.

I have invariably found this Warbler in swampy places,
generally on the edges of woods.

34. **Dendrœca virens**, BAIRD. — *Black-throated Green
Warbler.* Abundant during the migrations ; but breeds
commonly. Arrives from April 30th to May 19th ; departs in September. Found everywhere in the woods, but
generally among pine-trees.

* " The nest is rare, although I have seen half a dozen altogether " —
Professor S F. BAIRD in Epist.

35. **Dendrœca cœrulescens,** BAIRD. — *Black-throated Blue Warbler.* Rare during the migrations. Have taken it from May 15th to 24th. I have always found it in mixed woods. " Although not generally common, I found it quite plentiful during the season of 1869." *

36. **Dendrœca coronata,** GRAY. — *Yellow-rumped Warbler,* "Myrtle-Bird." Very abundant during the migrations. Arrives from April 20th to May 5th. I have seen it from April 18th until the 1st of June. Appears about the last week of September in great numbers, in straggling, detached flocks ; remains until November 1st. Perhaps some remain during the winter, at which time I have met with it in great numbers in Florida.

37. **Dendrœca castanea,** BAIRD. — *Bay-breasted Warbler.* Exceedingly rare. Possibly breeds, as I have taken a male on June 19, 1867. Arrives from May 17th to 22d. I have never met with this species in autumn. (See *D. striata.*) Mr. Brewster says that he has taken it in Wolfboro', New Hampshire, in May. Frequents the woods everywhere.

38. **Dendrœca Blackburniæ,** BAIRD. — *Mrs. Blackburn's Warbler, Blackburnian Warbler.* In some seasons not uncommon during the migrations. Arrives from May 17th to 27th ; departs for the south in September. Found everywhere, both in the woods and on apple-trees.

39. **Dendrœca pina,** BAIRD. — *Pine-creeping Warbler, Pine Warbler.* Common during the migrations. A few breed. Arrives from April 9th to 22d ; departs in September. Found everywhere.

40. **Dendrœca Pennsylvanica,** BAIRD. — *Chestnut-sided Warbler.* Common summer resident ; breeds commonly. Arrives from May 5th to 19th ; departs about the second week in September. Found everywhere.

41. **Dendrœca striata,** BAIRD. — *Black-polled War-*

* Mr. W. Brewster, in MS.

bler. Very abundant spring and autumn migrant. I have taken it in spring from May 15th until June 9th; in autumn, from September 19th until the latter part of October, — during this season it is very numerous. I think the *Sylvia autumnalis,* Wils., is really the young of this species. I have shot hundreds of this species in autumn, but have never taken one of the other (*D. castanea*).

42. **Dendrœca æstiva,** BAIRD. — *Summer Yellow-Bird.* The most common of the *Dendrœca* in summer; breeds abundantly. Arrives from April 30th to May 8th; departs early in September.

43. **Dendrœca maculosa,** BAIRD. — *Black and Yellow Warbler.* Rather rare migrant, although common during the spring of 1867. Arrives the third week in May; have taken it from the 23d to the 27th; have never met with it in autumn. Frequents the woods everywhere.

44. **Dendrœca palmarum,** BAIRD. — *Red-Poll Warbler,* "Palm Warbler.' Abundant during the migrations. I have taken it from April 9th to May 10th. In autumn it arrives from the north about the middle of September, and occupies about two weeks in passing. The most terrestrial of all the *Dendrœca.* Found everywhere.

45. **Dendrœca discolor,** BAIRD. — *Prairie Warbler.* Rather common summer resident. Arrives from May 13th to 19th. Frequents the high sandy fields grown up to bushes, or rocky hillside covered with barberry bushes, where it breeds. Has a most peculiar song, which is almost indescribable.

I have never met with the Blue Warbler (*Dendrœca cœrulea,* Baird) although it perhaps rarely occurs.

46. **Perissoglossa tigrina,** BAIRD. — *Cape May Warbler.* Exceedingly rare spring and autumn migrant. I have never met with it. Mr. W. Brewster has taken it in an apple-tree on May 17, 1867. The late Dr. Henry Bryant once showed me quite a number of skins, which he

said were taken in eastern Massachusetts, in spring, upon apple-trees when in bloom.

47. **Myiodioctes pusillus,** Bon. — *Black-capped Flycatching Warbler.* Not uncommon during the spring migrations. Have taken it from May 18th to 24th, but have never seen it in autumn. It sings well; has more of the habits of a Warbler than a Flycatcher. Frequents thickets, often by the side of a stream; I have also shot it on the tops of high trees.

48. **Myiodioctes Canadensis,** Aud. — *Canada Flycatching Warbler.* Common during the migrations. I have taken it from May 22d to June 4th. It is said to breed. Frequents low bushes on the edges of woods.

The Hooded Flycatching Warbler (*Myiodioctes mitratus,* Aud.) may occur, but I have yet to meet with a single well-authenticated instance of its capture.

49. **Setophaga ruticilla,** Swain. — *Redstart.* Common summer resident. Arrives from May 5th to 19th; last seen about September 10th. This species loves the deep woods, where it builds its nest, generally in the fork of a high limb, on some lofty tree.

HIRUNDINIDÆ, — The Swallows.

50. **Hirundo horreorum,** Barton. — *Barn Swallow.* Very abundant summer resident. Arrives the last week in April; departs in early September. Nests in barns.

51. **Petrochelidon lunifrons,** Cab. — *Cliff Swallow, Eaves Swallow.* Common summer resident. Arrives the first week in May; leaves in the latter part of August. Breeds under the eaves of barns, generally in associations, hundreds sometimes choosing one building; hence it is sometimes called the "Republican," or "Sociable Swallow." Formerly nested under cliffs.

52. **Tachycineta bicolor,** Cab. — *White-bellied Swal-*

5 *

low, "White-bellied Martin." Abundant summer resident. Arrives from March 31st to April 12th; the first of the Swallows in spring, also remaining the latest, departing about the middle of September. It congregates upon the salt marshes during the latter part of August and first of September literally by millions; the air is so completely filled with them that it is almost impossible to discharge a gun without killing some. Nests in the martin-houses, or in holes in buildings. I was extremely interested when, in company with my friend, Mr. Allen, we found a nest containing six eggs, built in the primitive manner, in a hole of an old blasted cedar-tree, upon the Ipswich Sand-hills. The tree had probably stood there for centuries.

53. **Cotyle riparia**, BOIE. — *Bank Swallow.* Abundant summer resident, especially along the coast. Arrives from May 13th to 21st; leaves the last week in August. Breeds by the thousand in the sandy banks along our shore, also in the interior. Both sexes assist in incubation.

54. **Progne subis**, BAIRD. — *Purple Martin,* "Black Martin." Common summer resident; somewhat local in its distribution; very abundant upon Cape Cod, while in some places in the interior it is rare. Arrives the last week in April; leaves about the last week in August.

VIREONIDÆ. — THE VIREOS.

55. **Vireo olivaceus**, VIEILL. — *Red-eyed Vireo.* Very abundant summer resident. Arrives from May 4th to 19th; leaves about the middle of September. Nests on trees in the woods, where it is always found.

56. **Vireo gilvus**, BON. — *Warbling Vireo.* Common summer resident. Arrives from May 8th to 16th; last

seen September 17th. Frequents orchards; seldom seen in the thick woods. Nests in trees, either in an orchard or among scattering forest-trees, never in the deep woods. This bird is easily distinguished from the other Vireos by its warbling and continuous song.

The "Brotherly-love Vireo" (*Vireo Philadelphicus*, Cass.) may occur as a rare summer visitor, as it has been taken in Maine.

57. **Vireo solitarius,** VIEILL. — *Blue-headed Vireo,* "Solitary Vireo." — Rather rare during the migrations. Arrives about the last week in April, passes quickly through; found again in September. Frequents the woods everywhere. Perhaps a few breed, for my friend, Mr. J. T. Brown, Jr., has taken it in June, at Concord, Massachusetts.

58. **Vireo flavifrons,** VIEILL. — *Yellow-throated Vireo.* Rather common summer resident. Arrives from May 9th to 15th; leaves about the first week in September. Frequents open woods and orchards, where it breeds, nesting on trees.

59. **Vireo noveboracensis,** BON. — *White-eyed Vireo.* Rather common summer resident in localities; rare in Newton, but common in the adjacent towns. Arrives from May 10th to 16th. Frequents swampy places, where it is somewhat difficult to procure, but is easily detected by its loud and peculiar notes. Breeds; builds its nest on the lower branch of a small tree, or on a low bush; it is generally hidden by the surrounding grass or foliage, and is difficult to find.

AMPELIDÆ, — THE WAXWINGS.

60. **Ampelis garrulus,** LINN. — *Bohemian Waxwing.* Accidental winter visitor from the north. The only instances of its capture in the eastern section of the State,

that I am aware of, occurred near Worcester, where several were taken; they were in the possession of Dr. Henry Bryant, of Boston; and Mr. J. A. Allen informs me that Mr. S. Jillson took several at Berlin a few years ago. Mr. William Brewster also saw a specimen, during November of 1869, at Watertown.

61. **Ampelis cedrorum**, BAIRD. — *Waxwing, Cedar-Bird*, "Cherry-Bird," "Canada Robin." Resident. Generally found through the winter; not always abundant, however. It becomes numerous in May, when it does considerable injury to the fruit of apple-trees by devouring the petals and stamens of the blossoms. It eats the small fruits, also a large number of insects, especially canker-worms, in the seasons when these pests rage. It breeds late, not until the middle of June. During the latter part of July it may be seen catching insects over ponds or streams. During September and October it disappears; but in November it reappears, and until the next spring feeds upon the berries of the cedar and mountain-ash. Gregarious at all times, it is, perhaps, less so during the breeding-season, at which time it is seen in small parties.

LANIIDÆ, — THE SHRIKES.

62. **Collurio borealis**, BAIRD. — *Great Northern Shrike.* Winter visitor, but somewhat irregular in numbers at various seasons. When the Lesser Red-Polls or the Pine Finches are common, the Shrikes follow them and prey upon them. Have known it to occur from October 6th to April 10th.

TANAGRIDÆ, — THE TANAGERS.

63. **Pyranga rubra**, VIEILL.—*Scarlet Tanager.* Rather common summer resident. Arrives from May 10th to 26th;

remains until the latter part of September. Found in open oak woods more plentifully during the spring migrations. Nests on the top of small trees.

64. **Pyranga æstiva**, VIEILL. — *Summer Tanager.* "Summer Red-Bird." Accidental. "Two were taken in Lynn after a severe storm, April 21, 1852."* I saw one in the collection of Mr. A. L. Babcock, at Sherborne, which was taken near that place; this specimen was a male in immature plumage. It has a loud and pleasing song.

FRINGILLIDÆ, — THE FINCHES AND SPARROWS.

65. **Pinicola Canadensis**, CAB. — *Pine Grosbeak.* An irregular winter visitant. On November 4, 1866, large numbers appeared, and remained through the winter, feeding upon the berries of the cedar; by February 27, 1867, it disappeared; it was also common during the winter of 1868–69.

The true reason of the visits of this northern bird is not, as many suppose, the severe winters, but its migrations are regulated entirely by the supply of food. While visiting northern Maine and New Hampshire in the autumn of 1868, I observed that the cone-bearing trees, upon the seeds of which this bird in a great measure subsists, had but few cones upon them; hence its abundance in Massachusetts during the succeeding winter. It is very unsuspicious, and may be taken with a noose upon a pole; is easily tamed, and will in a short time become quite familiar.

66. **Carpodacus purpureus**, GRAY. — *Purple Finch.* Abundant resident. Breeds, nesting in cedar-trees. Found during summer everywhere; during winter, among thick groves of cedar. Eagerly eats the petals and stamens

* S. Jillson, "Proceedings of the Essex Institute," I. p. 224.

of the apple-blossom; also eats a few insects; but generally feeds upon seeds. The plumage of the male of the first, second, and third years is gray like the female; on the fourth year it assumes the brighter male plumage. Both sexes sing, — the females not as loud as the males, however.

67. **Astragalinus tristis**, Cab. — *Goldfinch,* " Yellow-Bird," "Thistle-Bird." Abundant resident; gregarious in winter. Breeds late in June.

68. **Chrysomitris pinus**, Bon. — *Pine Linnet, Pine Finch.* — Another irregular winter visitor, whose movements are regulated by the supply of food, but in a different manner from *P. Canadensis;* it feeds upon the seeds of weeds a great deal during winter; in fact, they form its principal supply of food after the seeds of the birch are exhausted. When the snow is deep in the region north of Massachusetts, and covers the weeds to such a depth that they are not exposed, then we have a visit from this bird. It was very numerous during the winter of 1859 – 60, remaining until quite late; after that time I did not meet with it until the winter of 1868 – 69, when it was quite common; it remained until the last week in May. Its nest has been found at Cambridge.

69. **Ægiothus linarius**, Cab. — *Red-Poll, Lesser Red-Poll Linnet.* Irregular in its visits, and governed by the same laws as the preceding, with the exception that it is a more restless species. Common all the seasons that the preceding have been, and in the winter of 1866 – 67. Have taken it from the last of December until the 25th of April.

The *Ægiothus "exilipes"* of Coues (*Æ. canescens* of other ornithologists) is only a paler variety of this species, of which, if we admit the inconstant characters used in constructing it (*Æ. "exilipes"*) as tangible, we have an almost endless array of species.

70. **Curvirostra Americana,** Wils. — *Red Crossbill.*
Irregular in its visits ; the same laws regulate its appearance as govern *P. Canadensis,* and it is generally found the
same seasons. Frequents the pine woods. More numerous in the winter of 1862 – 63 than I have ever seen it
before ; it remained until April, when it was in full plumage and in full song. In the autumn of 1868 some interesting facts relative to the movements of this bird
came under my notice. During the latter part of August
it became quite numerous, and some specimens were in
immature plumage ; this would seem to indicate that it
breeds in Massachusetts. Upon going to Albany, Maine,
later in the season, I was informed, by the farmers, that
in August the Crossbill had appeared in great numbers,
and had done great damage to the oats by eating them
and cutting off the heads. When the oats were harvested,
it disappeared ; and at that time (October 12th) there was
not a single specimen to be found ! These were evidently
the birds that appeared in Massachusetts in the latter part
of August. Indeed, it passed *south* of Newton, Massachusetts, as upon my return, in November, not a bird
was to be found ! It breeds in *winter* in Maine, during
the month of February ; this statement is made upon the
authority of Mr. G. A. Boardman, who has taken their
nests and eggs at that time. It is also said to breed in
Massachusetts.

71. **Curvirostra leucoptera,** Wils. — *White-winged
Crossbill.* Being more northern in its habits than the preceding, it is seldom seen in this section. Common during the winter of 1868 – 69. On October 21st it appeared
in great numbers at Albany, Maine ; December 3d it was
found at Ipswich, Massachusetts, where it feeds upon the
seeds of the beach-grass ; a few days later it was seen in
Newton in large flocks. It remained until late in April.
Perhaps breeds. I obtained a specimen on June 13, 1866,

shot on an apple-tree in Newtonville; it was filled with canker-worms.

72. **Plectrophanes nivalis**, MEYER. — *Snow-Bunting*. Abundant winter visitor, especially on the sea-shore. I have seen thousands rise at the report of my gun, on the Ipswich Sand-hills, where it feeds upon the seeds of the beach-grass. This species, with the preceding four and *P. Canadensis*, are, while with us, always gregarious. Arrives in November; remains until April.

73. **Plectrophanes Lapponicus**, SELBY. — *Lapland Longspur, Lapland Bunting*. Generally rare, but common on the Ipswich Sand-hills, where it associates with the preceding; its note is different, being more shrill, but it has much the same habits. I have seen it with the Shore Larks, but have never met with it alone. Its proportion to the Snow-Bunting was about one in every hundred.

74. **Chondestes grammacus**, SWAIN. — *Lark Finch*. Exceedingly rare or accidental in autumn. One taken in Gloucester, in 1845, by S. Jillson.

75. **Centronyx Bairdii**, BAIRD. — *Baird's Sparrow*. It is with pleasure that I add this unique sparrow to the Catalogue of the Birds of Eastern Massachusetts. Previous to the capture of this there was but one specimen extant, which was one of the original birds captured by Audubon upon the banks of the Yellowstone River, July 26, 1843. My specimen, through the kindness of Professor S. F. Baird, has been compared with the original, which is in his possession, and pronounced identical; but as mine differs somewhat from his, I have thought best to give a description of it here. *

* " It differs in color just as clear autumnal birds differ from worn breeding ones, — tints paler, markings more suffused, etc. The stripe along the top of head is paler, not as fulvous as in the type ; but in all essential points it seems to be the same bird." — Professor S. F. BAIRD, in Epist.

Centronyx Bairdii, BAIRD. — *Baird's Sparrow.*

(See Frontispiece.*)

Emberiza Bairdii.   AUD., Birds America, VII. 1843 ; Pl. 500.
Coturniculus Bairdii. BON., Syn. 1850, 481.
Centronyx Bairdii.   BAIRD, Birds N. Am. 1858, 441.

SP. CH. — Back grayish ; the middle of the feathers having a black centre edged with rufous. Top of head streaked
with dusky and pale rufous, divided by a broad stripe of
pale yellowish white. There is also a whitish superciliary
stripe extending from the base of the bill to the back of
the head. Ear-coverts grayish, with a rufous tinge. Quills
brownish, edged with white on the outer web ; scapularies,
secondaries, and wing-coverts brownish-black, edged broad-
ly with rufous, brightest on the secondaries ; scapularies
also edged narrowly with white ; the ends of both rows of
wing-coverts narrowly tipped with white, forming two rather
indistinct bars across the wings. Tail brownish, with the
tips of the feathers and terminal half of the outer web of
the outer tail-feathers pale yellowish white ; the rest of the
tail-feathers narrowly edged with the same. Under parts,
incl ding under tail-coverts, pure white. Feathers of the
sides of the throat, with a broad band across the breast and
sides, streaked with rufous, with dusky centres. The throat'
is indistinctly spotted with dusky. A triangular spot on
the sides of the neck, below the ear-coverts, pale buff;
ears dusky. Bill dark brown, with the base of the under
mandible paler. Eyes and feet brown.

Differs from *Poœcetes gramineus*, which in general form it
resembles, in having a central stripe on the head, and a
general rufous appearance, also in having longer tarsi, toes,
and claws. With *Passerculus savanna* it cannot justly be
compared, as it is much larger, and has a shorter and more

* The convexity of the upper mandible is somewhat exaggerated in the
plate.

Measurements of C. Bairdii.

Catalogue No.	Sex	Locality.	When collected.	Length.	Stretch of Wing.	Wing.	Tail.	Bill above.	Bill along Gape.	Tarsus.	Middle Toe.	Claw of middle Toe.	Hind Toe and Claw.	Hind Claw.	Remarks.
1985	—	Fort Union, Neb.	Summer, 1843	4.64	—	2 77	2.10	0 49	0 50	0.84	0.73	0 18	0.72	0 84	Worn (?)
1744	♂	Ipswich, Mass.	Dec. 4, 1868	6.30	11.00	8 25	2.60	0.45	0.52	0.86	0.80	0 25	0.72	0 40	Perfect plumage.

obtuse bill. Indeed, so nearly does it resemble the *P. gramineus*, that amateur ornithologists to whom I have shown it have unhesitatingly pronounced it to be that species.

I give the comparative measurements of the two specimens, remarking that Professor Baird's was made from the dried skin, while mine was taken from the fresh bird.

The Ipswich Sand-hills, where the specimen was procured, is a most peculiar place. I never have met with its equal anywhere. Years ago these Sand-hills, which are three miles long by three fourths of a mile across, and contain about one thousand acres, were covered with a thick growth of pine-trees. Protected by these trees, and among them, dwelt a tribe of Indians, whose earlier presence is indicated, not only by tradition, but by numerous shell heaps scattered over the Sand-hills at irregular intervals. Indeed, even now the ashes of camp-fires may be seen, apparently fresh. Upon the advent of the white man, the usual event transpired, namely, the disappearance of the trees; and to-day, with the exception of a few scattering ones at the southeasterly corner, near the house of the proprietor of the Sand-hills, Mr. George Woodbury, not a tree is to be seen. All is bleak and barren. The surface of the ground, once covered with a slight deposit of soil, has become a mass of shifting sands. Many times has the present owner had cause to regret the want of foresight in his ancestors in removing the trees, as the several acres of arable land around the house are now covered with sand, including a valuable apple-orchard. Upon this orchard the sand has drifted to the depth of thirty feet. Some of the trees present the curious phenomenon of apples growing upon limbs that protrude a few feet only above the sand, while the trunk and lower branches are buried! The Sand-hills, in places, are covered with a sparse growth of coarse grass, upon the seeds of which,

as I have remarked elsewhere, thousands of Snow-Buntings feed.   There are, in some places, sinks or depressions
with the level of the sea.   In these sinks, which, except
during the summer months, are filled with fresh water,
a more luxuriant growth of grass appears.   Walking, on
December 4, 1868, near one of these places, in search of
Lapland Longspurs, I started a sparrow from out the tall
grass, which flew wildly, and alighted again a few rods
away.   I approached the spot, surprised at seeing a sparrow at this late day so far north, especially in so bleak a
place.   After some trouble I again started it.   It flew
wildly as before, when I fired, and was fortunate enough
to secure it.   It proved to be Baird's Sparrow.   When I
found I had taken a specimen which I had never seen before, — although at that time I did not know its name or
the interest attached to it, — I instantly went in search
of more.   After a time I succeeded in starting another.
This one, however, rose too far off for gunshot, and
I did not secure it.   It flew away to a great distance,
when I lost sight of it.   After this I thought that
among the myriads of Snow-Buntings that continually
rose a short distance from me I again detected it, but
I was perhaps mistaken.   I am confident of having
seen it in previous years at this place, earlier in the
season.

To show the similarity of the habits of these birds, even
in widely different localities, I give below extracts from
Audubon's account.   "During one of our buffalo hunts
(July 26, 1843) we happened to pass along several wet
places closely overgrown with a kind of slender, rush-like
grass, from which we heard the notes of this species, and
which we thought were produced by Marsh Wrens (*Troglodytes palustris*).   Messrs. Harris and J. G. Bell immediately
went in search of the birds.   Mr. Bell soon discovered that
the notes of Baird's Bunting were softer and more prolonged

than those of the Marsh Wren. They had some difficulty in starting them from the long and somewhat close grass to which this species seems to confine itself. Several times Mr. Bell nearly trod on them before the birds would take to wing; and they almost invariably alighted again within a few feet and ran like mice through the grass. . . . . After a while, two were shot on the wing. . . . . I have named this species in honor of my young friend, Spencer F. Baird, of Carlisle, Pennsylvania."

I think it more probable that the birds which occur at Ipswich are winter visitors from the north, than that they are stragglers from so great a distance as Nebraska. As might be expected, I heard no song-note at this season, but simply a short chirp of alarm.

76. **Passerculus savanna**, Bon. — *Savannah Sparrow.* Common summer resident; breeds abundantly along the coast, and sometimes in the interior. Have taken it from April 17th to November 12th. Frequents the fields and marshes.

77. **Poœcetes gramineus**, Baird. — *Bay-winged Sparrow,* "Grass Finch." Abundant; breeds in the fields everywhere. Arrives from April 5th to 20th; leaves about the 1st of November.

78. **Coturniculus passerinus**, Bon. — *Yellow-winged Sparrow.* Not an uncommon summer resident; breeds regularly. Arrives the first or second week in May; leaves early in September. Frequents dry sandy places, or pastures grown up to weeds. Very numerous on Nantucket Island, where it breeds abundantly.

79. **Coturniculus Henslowii**, Bon. — *Henslow's Sparrow.* Very rare summer resident. Took two males in a wet meadow on May 10, 1867. Song-note like the syllables "see'-wick," with the first prolongedly and the second quickly given. Said to breed. Mr. J. A. Allen informs me that the specimens that he has taken have been

found in the same situation as the preceding species, namely, sandy fields.

80. **Zonotrichia leucophrys,** SWAIN. — *White-crowned Sparrow.* Very rare migrant. Took a female on May 27, 1869, in a swampy thicket by the roadside. I have heard of but few instances of its capture in this section.

81. **Zonotrichia albicollis,** BON. — *White-throated Sparrow.* Common during the migrations. Have taken it from April 27th until May 20th, and from about September 1st to October 19th. Frequents the low bushes and swampy thickets.

82. **Ammodromus maritimus,** SWAIN. — *Sea-side Finch.* Said to occur commonly along the coast of our State, which statement I doubt, as I have searched carefully for it from the mouth of the Merrimack River to the extreme south shore, and have yet to meet with a single living specimen; neither does it occur on the Island of Nantucket to my knowledge. Dr. Coues says it is abundant in New Hampshire on the coast. It may rarely occur on our coast during the migrations. Mr. Brewster informs me that he has looked for it in vain at Rye Beach, New Hampshire.

83. **Ammodromus caudacutus,** SWAIN. — *Sharp-tailed Finch.* Not common. I know of but one locality where this bird is to be found; that is, on the salt marshes of Charles River. I have taken it there in the latter part of June. It is difficult to procure, as it lies close, and has to be shot while on the wing. It instantly conceals itself in the grass when it alights. Mr. Brewster informs me that it breeds late, — the first week in July. Remains late. "Have taken it in the marshes of Charles River the last week in October." * Since writing the above, I have found it quite common on the marshes at Ipswich during the last week in September, 1869.

* J. A. Allen, " Proceedings of the Essex Institute," IV. 1864, p. 84.

84. **Junco hyemalis**, SCLATER. — *Snow-Bird.* Common winter visitant; abundant in spring and autumn. Have taken it from October 14th to May 20th. Found everywhere.

85. **Spizella monticola**, BAIRD. — *Tree Sparrow.* Common winter visitor; more abundant in spring and autumn. Have taken it from November 2d to April 25th. Seen everywhere, and with the preceding frequents cedar woods in winter.

86. **Spizella socialis**, BON. — *Chipping Sparrow.* Abundant summer resident. Found breeding everywhere. Arrives from April 10th to 21st; leaves about the middle of October. The most familiar and sociable of all our Sparrows, hopping about our doors, and even entering houses in search of food.

87. **Spizella pusilla**, BON. — *Field Sparrow.* Common summer resident; breeds on low bushes in high sandy places, and rocky fields grown up to bushes. Arrives from April 14th to 27th; found in flocks with the preceding in autumn, and departs at the same time.

88. **Melospiza melodia**, BAIRD. — *Song Sparrow.* Abundant summer resident. Comes earlier and remains later than any of the summer Sparrows. Arrives from February 20th to March 18th; I have taken it on the 3d of December. Mr. Brewster informs me that he has taken it every month in the year; has even heard it sing in January.

89. **Melospiza palustris**, BAIRD. — *Swamp Sparrow.* Common summer resident. Frequents bushy swamps and marshes, and breeds in them. Arrives from March 27th to April 14th; departs about the middle of November. It is probable that Audubon was mistaken when he said that this bird was common *in winter* about Boston. It has a peculiar, and not particularly pleasing, song during the breeding-season; but in autumn I have

heard it sing with a low warbling note which was very pleasant.

90. Melospiza Lincolnji, BAIRD. — *Lincoln's Sparrow.* Very rare. Mr. S. Jillson has taken it at Hudson on one or two occasions in spring.

91. Passerella iliaca, SWAIN. — *Fox-colored Sparrow.* Common during the migrations. Have taken it in spring from March 14th to April 13th. While with us at this season it has a most pleasing song. Passes us in the autumn in October.

92. Passer domestica, LEACH. — *European House Sparrow.* Introduced, but common already in localities ; will soon, without doubt, be generally distributed.

93. Euspiza Americana, BON. — *Black-throated Bunting.* Very rare summer visitor, or straggler, from the south. My young friend, John Thaxter, shot a specimen June 26, 1867 ; it was a female, and, as I should judge, from the peculiar appearance of the ovaries and oviduct, had laid her eggs ; while the bare and swollen appearance of her breast seemed to indicate that she was incubating. Mr. Samuels speaks of two instances of its capture.*

94. Guiraca Ludoviciana, SWAIN. — *Rose-breasted Grosbeak.* Common summer resident. Breeds, nesting in trees and bushes. Arrives from May 8th to 22d ; leaves early in September. Frequents open woods.

The Blue Grosbeak (*Guiraca cærulea*, Swain.) perhaps rarely occurs ; it has been taken in Calais, Maine, "where it is very uncertain, but was common in the spring of 1861."†

95. Cyanospiza cyanea, BAIRD. — *Indigo-Bird.* Common summer resident. Breeds, nesting in low bushes. Arrives from May 10th to 22d ; in autumn found in flocks

---

* " Ornithology and Oölogy of New England," p 328.

† G. A. Boardman, " Proceedings of the Boston Society of Natural History," IX. p. 127; J. A. Allen, " Proceedings of the Essex Institute," IV. 1864, pp. 84, 85.

with other Sparrows. Frequents roadsides, high sandy fields, and rocky pastures.

The Cardinal, "Red-Bird" (*Cardinalis Virginianus*, Bon.), according to Nuttall, occurs accidentally. I have never met with it in this section.

96. **Pipilo ery.hrophthalmus**, Vieill. — *Towhee Bunting*, "Ground Robin," "Chewink." Common summer resident. Breeds commonly, nesting on the ground among low bushes, which it frequents. Arrives from April 28th to May 10th; leaves by the first week in October.

ALAUDIDÆ, — The Larks.

97. **Eremophila alpestris**, Forster. — *Shore Lark.* Common winter resident. Perhaps a few breed. Seen by Mr. W. Brewster, in July, 1869. Arrives early in the autumn. Have seen it in spring as late as April 25th. Frequents the ploughed fields, beaches, and marshes. Has the habit of hiding in holes or beside stones.

ICTERIDÆ, — The Orioles, Starlings, etc.

98. **Dolichonyx oryzivorus**, Swain. — *Bob-o-link,* "Rice-Bird," "Reed-Bird." Abundant summer resident. Breeds, nesting in the grass on the ground. Arrives from April 30th to May 12th. During the first of September it congregates in flocks of immense numbers upon the sea-shore; at this time both sexes are in the same plumage. It is then shot for the table. While migrating, it moves night and day; indeed, almost any clear night in August its metallic-like note may be heard high up in the air.

99. **Molothrus pecoris**, Swain. — *Cow-Bird*, "Cow-

6

Bunting." Common summer resident. Arrives from April 6th to 19th; leaves by the last week in October. Deposits its eggs in the nests of other birds, — the only example of polygamy among undomesticated birds in North America. Gregarious throughout the year, but more so in autumn. Often seen around cows in pursuit of insects, sometimes alighting upon them; from this habit it derives its popular (Cow-Bunting) and specific (*pecoris*) names.

100. **Agelæus Phœniceus**, VIEILL. — *Red-winged Blackbird*, "Swamp Blackbird." Common summer resident. Arrives from February 25th to March 10th; leaves by the last of October. Nests in the marshes, generally on a tussock; sometimes in low bushes. I have found the nests on an island in the marshes of Essex River, placed on trees twenty feet from the ground! In one case, where the nest was placed on a slender sapling fourteen feet high, that swayed with the slightest breeze, the nest was constructed after the manner of our Baltimore Orioles, prettily woven of the bleached sea-weed called eel-grass. So well constructed was this nest, and so much at variance with the usual style, that had it not been for the female sitting on it, I should have taken it for a nest of *I. Baltimore*. It was six inches deep.

101. **Xanthocephalus icterocephalus**, BAIRD. — *Yellow-headed Blackbird*. A single specimen was procured by my young friend, Frank Sanger, at Watertown, about the 15th of October, 1869. The wings, tail, and one foot of this specimen are now in my possession. Through the kindness of Mr. J. A. Allen, I have been enabled to compare them with specimens of the same species in the Museum of Comparative Zoölogy, thereby identifying them. This bird was in immature plumage, evidently the young-of-the-year. It was shot in an orchard. The occurrence of this specimen in this section is singular, as its usual

habitat is in the West; its range eastward being about the longitude of Chicago.

102. **Sturnella magna,** SWAIN. — *Meadow Lark*, "Marsh Quail." Resident; common in summer, but few winter here. Breeds in old fields. Gregarious in autumn and winter.

103. **Icterus Baltimore,** DAUDIN. — *Baltimore Oriole*, "Golden Robin," "Fire Hang-Bird." Very common summer resident. Arrives from May 5th to 12th; leaves about the middle of September. Breeds, nesting generally on tall trees. I have heard a bird of this species that lived among the woods of the islands in Essex River, where man is seldom seen, sing with a louder, wilder note than usual, as if it was influenced by the surrounding wildness and its proximity to the sounding sea. This is the only bird that I have met with which will readily devour the tent caterpillar.

104. **Icterus spurius,** BON. — *Orchard Oriole*, "Spurious Oriole." Generally a rare summer resident, but quite common in the spring of 1865; I saw a few in 1866. Arrives about May 18th. Mr. Brewster says that he finds a pair or two breeding every season.

105. **Scolecophagus ferrugineus,** SWAIN. — *Rusty Grakle*, "Rusty Blackbird." Common spring and autumn migrant. Arrives from March 8th to 30th, remains into April; arrives from the North the last week in September, remaining into November. Very unsuspicious, and frequents the bushes by the side of water. Generally seen in small flocks, sometimes in company with the succeeding species.

106. **Quiscalus versicolor,** VIEILL. — *Purple Grakle*, "Crow Blackbird." Common summer resident. Arrives from March 1st to 20th; remains into November. Breeds in communities, generally nesting in tall trees; but I have found its nest on the islands in the Essex River, on bushes

six feet high.   Other nests on the same islands were placed in trees, from twenty to forty feet from the ground.

CORVIDÆ, — The Crows.

107. Cyanura cristata, Swain. — *Blue Jay.*   Common resident.   Nests in trees.   Is a general nuisance ; destroys the young and eggs of small birds; visits the cornfields of the farmer in autumn, and carries away great quantities of corn.   Gregarious throughout the year, except during the breeding-season.

108. Corvus Americanus, Aud. — *Crow.* Common resident.   Nests in trees.   Appears on the sea-shore in great numbers during the early winter, and continues until spring, feeding upon the refuse left by the tide upon the marshes.   These winter visitors are said to be "Eastern Crows," or crows from Maine and the British Provinces.

TYRANNIDÆ, — The Tyrant Flycatcher.

109. Tyrannus Carolinensis, Baird. — *King-Bird,* "Bee Martin." —Common summer resident.   Breeds, nesting on trees, generally in an orchard.   Arrives from May 6th to 15th ; leaves about the middle of September.   Frequents open fields and orchards.

110. Tyrannus Dominicensis, Rich. — *Gray King-Bird.*   An immature specimen was taken by Mr. Charles Goodall, at Lynn, on October 23, 1868.   The bird is now in the possession of Mr. N. Vickery.   It was shot upon a tree near the roadside.   The occurrence of this specimen is a striking illustration of the straggling habits of some individuals among birds, its usual habitat being Florida and the West Indies.

111. **Myiarchus crinitus**, Cab. — *Great Crested Fly-catcher*. Very rare summer resident. Have taken it on May 9th and 15th. Said to breed. Frequents the open woods.

112. **Sayornis fuscus**, Baird. — *Phœbe, Pewee*. Common summer resident. Arrives from March 25th to April 12th. Have taken it as late as October 9th. Nests in barns, under bridges, and under some projecting rock of a ledge; in the spring it may be found in the neighborhood of these localities, but it occurs everywhere in autumn. Although a strictly insectivorous bird, yet, when compelled by hunger, it can be granivorous; during a violent snow-storm, April 2, 1868, I shot one whose stomach was completely filled with the seeds of the berries of the hawthorn (*Cratægus oxycantha*).

113. **Contopus borealis**, Baird. — *Olive-sided Fly-catcher*. Not a very rare summer resident. Breeds. " Nests generally in the fork of a pine-tree; the only nest that I ever found that was not placed in this situation was on the outer limb of an apple-tree." * Frequents the open wood. Arrives from May 12th to 24th; leaves early in September.

114. **Contopus virens**, Cab. — *Wood Pewee*. Common summer resident. Arrives from May 19th to 28th; leaves early in September. Breeds. The nest is composed of moss, and is placed on the top of some high limb, and resembles a protuberance upon it; for this reason it is not easily detected. Frequents open woods.

If the Acadian Flycatcher (*Empidonax Acadicus*, Baird) is found in eastern Massachusetts, I have yet to meet with it. I think that this and the following are often confounded by collectors, perhaps with good reason.

115. **Empidonax Traillii**, Baird. — *Traill's Fly-catcher*. Rare in spring; said to breed, however. I have

* MS. Notes of W. Brewster.

met with it but once, — on June 1, 1869, in a swampy thicket; it was very shy. I heard no note.

116. **Empidonax minimus**, BAIRD. — *Least Fly-catcher.* Common summer resident. Breeds. Arrives from April 22d to May 5th; leaves about the middle of September. Seen everywhere. Specimens differ in the intensity of the olivaceous green upon the back; those which are found in the woods are much darker than those which inhabit the orchards or straggling trees, these being often quite gray. They are also exceedingly variable in size.

117. **Empidonax flaviventris**, BAIRD. — *Yellow-bellied Flycatcher.* On May 31, 1869, I shot the first specimen I had ever seen living; the next day (June 1st) I took *eight* of both sexes in a few hours! Between this time and the 10th I took two or three more. I do not doubt that it has occurred in previous seasons, but, being unaccustomed to its low note, — which is like the syllable *Pea* very plaintively and prolongedly given, — and its retiring habits, I had not detected it before. The specimens captured were all, with the exception of the first, — which was shot on a tall oak, — taken in low, swampy thickets. It keeps near the ground, is rather shy, and upon the appearance of the intruder instantly ceases its song. "Shot a specimen on May 25, 1869, in Watertown, singing, with its peculiar note, *in an apple-tree.* I have shot the *female singing* in the same manner, in August, 1867, in Franconia, New Hampshire. The only note I ever heard was the low *Pea*." *

I have yet to hear the "pleasing song" attributed to this species and other members of the genus. I think that the anatomical structure of the throat and larynx is not of the complicated character seen in singing-birds; and therefore consider it a physical impossibility for members of this genus to produce a *variety* of melodious notes.

* MS. Notes of W. Brewster.

ALCEDINIDÆ, — The Kingfishers.

118. **Ceryle alcyon**, Boie.—*Belted Kingfisher.* Common summer resident. Breeds. Frequents the neighborhood of streams and ponds. Arrives from March 21st to April 11th; remains into November; but I never have seen it in winter, at which time it may rarely occur.

CAPRIMULGIDÆ, — The Goatsuckers.

119. **Antrostomus vociferus**, Boie. — *Whippoorwill.* Common in the wild districts, where its rapid but indescribably mournful notes may be heard in the evening twilight. It also sings in the early dawn. Arrives from May 19th to 24th. Breeds, nesting on the ground.

120. **Chordeiles popetue**, Baird. — *Night-Hawk.* "Bull Bat." Common summer resident. Breeds, nesting on the ground. Arrives from April 7th to May 23d. Much more diurnal in its habits than the preceding, often seen flying about at midday. By the latter part of August it migrates in large, straggling flocks, moving day and night. While at rest in the daytime, it usually sits longitudinally upon a large limb of a tree; the peculiar structure of its feet rendering it impossible for it to clasp the limb and sit transversely, as is usual with other birds.

CYPSELIDÆ, — The Swifts.

121. **Chætura pelasgia**, Steph. — *Chimney Swift,* "Chimney Swallow." Abundant summer resident. Breeds, nesting in unused flues in chimneys. Arrives from May 1st to 11th; have seen it as late as September 14th.

TROCHILIDÆ, — The Humming-Birds,

122. **Trochilus colubris,** Linn. — *Ruby-throated Humming-Bird.* Common summer resident. Breeds, nesting in trees. Arrives about the second week in May; have seen it as late as the 23d of September.

123. **Argytira maculata,** Cab. and Heine. — *Linnæus's Emerald.* A single specimen of this beautiful little bird was captured by Mr. William Brewster, at Cambridge, in August, 1864; it was moulting, and apparently a female. How this little stranger should have come so far from its usual habitat, which is northern South America, is a mystery, and an event unheard of before. It certainly could not have been caged, and in *that* manner brought here, as it would not survive the passage.

I have carefully examined into the history of this specimen, and there seems no reason to doubt its being captured in Cambridge.

CUCULIDÆ, — The Cuckoos.

124. **Coccygus Americanus,** Bon. — *Yellow-billed Cuckoo.* Irregular in its visits; during the summer of 1866 it was very numerous, while the following species was rare; since then this has been rare, while the other is common. Arrives from May 18th to 23d. Frequents the woods and orchards.

125. **Coccygus erythrophthalmus,** Bon. — *Black-billed Cuckoo.* Rather common. (See remarks under *C. Americanus.*) Frequents the woods and orchards. The note of this species is not perhaps as harsh as the other. They are both inveterate destroyers of birds' eggs. They frequently sing at night. Both depart early in September.

PICIDÆ, — THE WOODPECKERS.

126. **Picus villosus,** LINN. — *Hairy Woodpecker.* Resident; but not common in winter, and rare in summer. I am confident that the specimens of this and the following species seen in winter do not come from the far north, or even from northern Maine and New Hampshire, for this reason: specimens shot in the sections above mentioned have the white terminal portion of the tail stained by the bark of the hemlock and other evergreen trees, upon which they climb in search of food, with an *indelible,* bright rufous or ochre color; this color is never seen on specimens taken here, even during severe winters. They must be resident individually by this infallible proof.

127. **Picus pubescens,** LINN. — *Downy Woodpecker.* Resident. Abundant throughout the winter, not uncommon in summer.

128. **Picoides arcticus,** GRAY. — *Black-backed Three-toed Woodpecker.* Exceedingly rare winter visitor. There are a male and female in the museum of the Peabody Academy of Science, at Salem, taken on November 21, 1855, in Essex County, by S. Jillson.

129. **Picoides hirsutus,** GRAY. — *Banded Three-toed Woodpecker.* Exceedingly rare winter visitor. Mr. Allen informs me that Mr. G. O. Welch took a pair in Lynn.

130. **Sphyrapicus varius,** BAIRD. — *Yellow-bellied Woodpecker.* Not common during the migrations. Frequents open woods. I do not think it breeds.

131. **Melanerpes erythrocephalus,** SWAIN. — *Red-headed Woodpecker.* Exceedingly rare summer visitor, perhaps accidental. I have never seen it living. A male taken by S. Jillson, in Essex County, in 1855. One seen by Mr. W. Brewster, in summer, at Waltham.

132. **Colaptes auratus,** SWAIN. — *Golden-winged Wood-*

6 *   I

pecker, " Pigeon Woodpecker," " Yellow-Hammer," " Wood-
wall," " Flicker," " Sucker," " High-holder," " Wake-up."
Common resident. Breeds, nesting in holes in trees. Arrives early, about the 1st of April ; remains until October
30th. A few remain all winter in the thick cedar woods.
Frequents open woods and orchards ; in autumn is seen in
cornfields, at which season it is partly gregarious, but it is
always a sociable bird, preferring the company of its species to solitude. Generally feeds upon ants or their larvæ
and eggs.

STRIGID.E, — THE OWLS.

133. **Strix pratincola,** BON. — *Barn Owl.* Mr. Vickery informs me that he mounted a specimen that was
taken in Lynn during the autumn of 1865. This is the
first authentic instance of its capture in this section. Mr.
Allen also informs me that it has been taken at Springfield.

134. **Otus Wilsonianus,** AUD. — *Long-eared Owl.* Rather common resident in this section. Breeds. Frequents
dark swamps and thick evergreen woods. This and the
following species are almost entirely destitute of sight during the brighter light of day.

135. **Brachyotus Cassinii,** BREW. — *Short-eared Owl.*
Common resident. Breeds. Frequents low bushes along
the sea-shore in the daytime ; starts up suddenly when approached, flies a short distance in a dazed, irregular manner, and then alights. Also frequents cedar woods. More
common on the sea-shore than in the interior.

136. **Syrnium cinereum,** AUD. — *Great Gray Owl.*
Rare winter visitor. Two specimens in the museum of
the Peabody Academy of Science, — one taken during the
winter of 1866–67, by F. W. Putnam, in Salem ; another,
by James Bartlett, in Wenham, in February, 1859.

137. **Syrnium nebulosum**, GRAY. — *Barred Owl.*
Common resident. Frequents the thick woods everywhere. May be approached closely on a bright day, as
it is then almost deprived of sight.

138. **Bubo Virginianus**, BON. — *Great Horned Owl.*
Rather common resident. Frequents the thick woods.
Sees well in the daylight, and is difficult to approach.

139. **Scops asio,** *Mottled Owl,* " Red Owl," " Screech
Owl." Common resident ; nests in holes in trees. Very
variable in plumage, on which account many have supposed there were two species. Mr. W. Brewster records
in the August number of the American Naturalist, 1869,
an instance of the young of a red mother being *red* and
gray; the red one *being quite rufous, even when in the down,*
and perceptibly different from the other. My young friend,
Frank Sanger, has also two young, both from the same
nest, one of which is red and the other gray ; *there was no
difference in plumage, however, when they were both in the
down.* Out of eight young which have fallen into my hands,
not one has been red. I have also a specimen in my possession, which I shot at Jullington, on the St. John's River in
Florida, which exactly divides these stages, or possesses both
colors so nicely blended and mixed that it is impossible to
decide which predominates. These cases alone prove that
we must look for other characters on which to base our
specific claims than merely the red and gray stages of
plumage. Throwing aside the claims that the red and
gray stages present as separate specific distinctions, is
there any rule that we can fix for this change of plumage ? I think not ; further than the supposition — which
I have not yet seen proven — that perfectly mature birds
may all agree in color. But while under one year old
the gray seems to be the normal stage, and the red the
unusual stage. Out of twenty young-of-the-year specimens of this species that have come under my personal

observation, I have seen but *three* in the *red* plumage.
On the other hand, among more mature birds, I have,
out of perhaps forty specimens personally examined, found
but *four* or *five* in the *gray!* Mr. Allen informs me that
although such formerly was his experience, latterly he has
met with many more *gray* than *red* birds. By these evidences I have become fully convinced that in the earlier
stages — perhaps to the third year — the coloration of
the plumage of *Scops asio* is exceedingly variable as a
species and somewhat individually, but in this last re-
spect it is more constant. The only doubt that now remains is, Do birds of a certain age or period all assume
some particular plumage as a final one? I am now inclined
to think they do. Perhaps the final stage is *gray;* but
this, as I said before, yet remains to be proven. It seems
to be an imperative law of nature for birds, — no matter
how variable and inconstant their plumages in earlier
stages may have been, — at some age or period to assume a final one, with the specific characters variable in
a comparatively small degree, as heretofore pointed out.

This inconstancy of plumage is also illustrated in the
young of the Cedar-Bird (*Ampelis cedrorum*); mature specimens of this species always have the peculiar, sealing-wax-
like, horny expansions of the shaft of the feathers on the
tips of the secondaries, and sometimes on the tips of the
tail-feathers. In the younger stages many are destitute
of them. I have, however, detected it upon the secondaries, and even upon the tails, of birds in the nesting plumage.

With these facts to guide us, we can but adopt the
above hypothesis relative to the final assumption of some
particular plumage by *Scops asio*, until it has been proven
that this is an exception to the governing and heretofore
unchanging law of nature.

This bird sees as well in the daytime as in the night.

It is easily tamed, and may be allowed to go and come at will, without fear of its taking its departure. I have one in my possession that returns to rest in the daytime, either in a building or on the trees near it, where I feed him daily.

140. **Nyctale Acadica,** Bon. — *Acadian Owl.* Rare resident; perhaps less so in winter. In September, 1867, while encamped for the night upon the banks of Popalatic Pond, in Medway, Massachusetts, I heard the peculiar rasping notes of this species. There were several. Evidently attracted by the light of our camp-fire, they came directly overhead, alighting on the tall poplar-trees; but as they remained in the impenetrable gloom that always surrounds one who is by a fire, especially in the woods in the open air at night, we were unable to secure a specimen.

141. **Nyctale Richardsonii,** Bon. — *Richardson's Owl.* Very rare. Mr. William Brewster has a fine specimen in his cabinet, taken at Mount Auburn, in December, 1865. "A specimen in the Museum of Comparative Zoölogy, Cambridge, taken at Malden." *

142. **Nyctea nivea,** Gray. — *Snowy Owl.* Not uncommon on the coast; rare in the interior during winter. Sees very well in the daytime; is shy, and difficult to approach.

143. **Surnia ulula,** Bon. — *Hawk Owl.* Very rare winter visitor. I have seen it but once.

FALCONIDÆ, — The Eagles, Falcons, and Hawks.

144. **Aquila Canadensis,** Cass. — *Golden Eagle.* "Ring-tailed Eagle." Perhaps rarely occurs as a transient visitor. A specimen in the museum of the Peabody Academy of Science, at Salem, labelled "Essex Co." Mr. Allen

* J. A. Allen, "Proceedings of the Essex Institute," IV. 1864, p. 52.

says it has been taken at "Lexington, near Boston, and at Upton, in 1849." No record of its very recent capture, however, in this section. I have never met with it.

145. **Haliaetus leucocephalus,** SAVIG. — *White-headed Eagle*, "Bald Eagle." Not uncommon on the sea-shore. I do not think it breeds *now*, but it *did* twenty-five or thirty years ago.

146. **Pandion Carolinensis,** BON. — *Fish-Hawk.* Not a common summer resident, growing less so every year. Perhaps a few breed in the interior, but it is doubtful.

147. **Falco anatum,** BON. — *American Penguin Falcon*, "Duck Hawk," "Great-footed Hawk." Rare visitor. I do not think it breeds ; no instance on record of its doing so in this section. This species seems to prefer the more mountainous regions, especially during the breeding-season.

148. **Falco sacer,** FORSTER. — *Jerfalcon*, "White Hawk." Very rare during winter, perhaps accidental. I have seen this species but once, — November 4, 1868, — flying high above the snow-topped mountains of New Hampshire, steering northward over the unbroken forests, — even thus early in the season covered with snow, and almost a solitude, — deserted by nearly all of the feathered tribe.

149. **Falco columbarius,** GM. — *Pigeon Hawk.* Not an uncommon resident. I think it breeds, as I have a specimen taken during the breeding-season, with all the evidences of its incubating. Perhaps more uncommon during winter.

150. **Falco sparverius,** LINN. — *Sparrow Hawk.* Not a very common resident. Breeds.

151. **Astur atricapillus,** BON. — *Goshawk*, "Partridge Hawk," "Blue Hawk." Not uncommon in winter. Some few undoubtedly breed. A pair remained in Weston, near a heavily wooded district, during the breeding-

season (1868); they evidently had a nest in the immediate vicinity. I have seen specimens taken in Massachusetts in full plumage quite frequently.

152. **Accipiter Cooperii**, Bon. — *Cooper's Hawk.* One
of the most common Hawks, called everywhere "Chicken
Hawk." Summer resident. I do not think any remain
during winter. Breeds, nesting in trees.

153. **Accipiter fuscus**, Bon. — *Sharp-shinned Hawk,*
" Pigeon Hawk." Common summer resident. Breeds.

154. **Buteo borealis**, Vieill. — *Red-tailed Buzzard,*
"Red-tailed Hawk." Common resident; exceedingly trouble-
some to farmers. This and *B. lineatus* are the well-known
and formidable " Hen-Hawks." Nests in tall trees.

155. **Buteo lineatus**, Jar. — *Red-shouldered Buzzard,*
"Red-shouldered Hawk," "Hen Hawk." Common resident; usually more abundant in this immediate locality in
winter than during any other season. Breeds, nesting in
tall trees, generally in swampy places.

The following is a description of a Hawk of this species
which is remarkably light-colored. This specimen is so
different from others of the same species that it was at
first supposed to be the *Buteo Cooperii*, Cass., and was mentioned as such by Mr. J. A. Allen.* This specimen is also
much larger than the average, as will be seen by the table
of measurements, and was evidently an *immature* bird,
which corroborates the rule given in the Introduction (p.
84) relative to birds decreasing in size with age.

Description of a light-colored specimen of B. lineatus.†

Bill not very large, slightly lobed on the upper mandible ; color, dark brown. Upper parts dark brown, with
each feather spotted and barred irregularly with white and
pale rufous, the latter colors predominating on the head

* " American Naturalist," III. p. **519.**

† Taken from a mounted specimen

and rump. Quills also dark brown, irregularly barred, and
edged with rufous Tail, on the upper parts, brown, lighter
beneath, tipped with dirty white, and with about twelve irregular transverse bars of pale rufous, white at base above
and below. Under parts generally, with the exception of
the under wing-coverts, — which are rufous — and the tips
of the quills — which are dark brown, — pale buff, becoming almost white on the under tail-coverts, with a few
scattering sagittate and cordate spots of reddish brown on
the breast and sides. Stripes running from the gape down
the side of the neck, and a narrow one on the chin and
upper part of the throat brown. There is a pale buff
superciliary stripe. Lores dusky mixed with white ; tibiæ
pale rufous, *unspotted ;* tarsi long and slender, entirely
naked behind, feathered down about an inch in front.
There are thirteen transverse scales in front, and sixteen
behind. The scales end abruptly in front and behind, on
the lower part of the tarsi, also on the upper part in front;
but behind they run greatly into smaller quinquangular
scales ; feet not very strong ; claws much curved, and
proportionate to the size of the feet.

Measurement of B. lineatus

Locality.	Date.	Length (about).	Stretch.	Wing.	Tail.	Bill.	Tarsus.	Middle Toe and Claw.	Middle Claw alone.	Hind Toe and Claw.	Hind Claw alone.
Cambridge	1866. Nov. 17	22.00	—	14.75	9 50	0.90	2.75	1.90	0.75	2.10	0.95

The specimen was shot among a thick growth of small
pines, beeches, etc., in a swampy place.

156. **Buteo Pennsylvanicus**, Bon. — *Broad-winged Buzzard,* " Broad-winged Hawk," " Hen-Hawk." Not very common. I have never seen it in winter. Perhaps breeds.

157. **Archibuteo lagopus**, Gray. — *Rough-legged Hawk.* Rare winter visitor. Rather sluggish in its habits.

158. **Archibuteo Sancti-Johannis**, Gray. — *Black Hawk.* A magnificent specimen of this handsome Hawk was sent to me by Mr. J. F. Le Baron, of Ipswich; it was killed while flying over the marshes. This is the only instance that I can record of its capture in this section.

159. **Circus Hudsonicus**, Vieill. — *Marsh Hawk.* Common summer resident. Breeds, nesting on the ground.

160. **Cathartes aura**, Illig. — *Turkey Vulture,* " Turkey Buzzard." Accidental. " Two specimens shot in the State in 1863." A gentleman who is perfectly familiar with the appearance of this bird informs me that he saw a specimen flying over the meadows at Waltham in August, 1867.

161. **Cathartes atratus**, Les. — *Black Vulture,* "Black-headed Buzzard." Accidental. "One was obtained at Swampscott, in November, 1850. Another was taken the past season (September 28), at Gloucester, by Mr. William Huntsford." *

COLUMBIDÆ, — The Pigeons.

162. **Ectopistes migratorius**, Swain. — *Wild Pigeon.* Still common in localities, but growing less so every year. Generally seen in autumn ; but a few winter.

163. **Zenædura Carolinensis**, Bon. — *Dove,* "Turtle Dove," "Carolina Dove." Not uncommon. Breeds commonly at Cape Cod, early in the season.

* J. A. Allen, " Proceedings of the Essex Institute," IV. 1864, p. 81.

TETRAONIDÆ, — The Grouse.

164. Tetrao Canadensis, LINN. — *Spruce Partridge.*
Accidental. " Found in the hemlock woods of Gloucester,
in September, 1851." *

165. Bonasa umbellus, STEPH. — *Ruffed Grouse,*
" Partridge." Common in the wilder sections; but from
the persecutions of sportsmen rapidly becoming extinct.
In localities where ten or fifteen years ago they were abundant not one can be found to-day. Nests on the ground
in moist woods.

166. Cupidonia cupido, BAIRD. — *Pinnated Grouse,*
" Prairie Hen." Said once to have been common in Massachusetts, but now has become extinct on the main-land;
still may be found in small numbers on the islands of
Martha's Vineyard and Naushon.

PERDICIDÆ, — The Partridges.

167. Ortyx virginiana, BON. —*Quail.* Resident; common in localities, but rapidly becoming extinct. Breeds,
nesting on the ground.

CHARADRIIDÆ, — The Plovers.

168. Charadrius Virginicus, BORCK. —*Golden Plover,*
" Green Plover," " Three-toed Plover," " Black-back,"
" Pale-bellied Plover," " Frost-Bird." Common spring and
autumn migrant. Frequents the hills near the sea-shore.

169. Ægialitis vociferus, CASS. — *Killdeer Plover.*
Rather rare summer resident. Said to have been common
years ago in localities.

* S. Jillson, "Proceedings of the Essex Institute," I. p. 224.

170. **Ægialitis semipalmatus**, Cab. — *Ring Plover.*
" Ring-Neck," " Ox-eye.'   Abundant on the shore during
the migrations.

171. **Ægialitis melodus**, Cab. — *Piping Plover,*
" Ring-Neck."   Common summer resident.   Breeds abun·
dantly in June on the sandy shores.

The Wilson's Plover, " Ring-Neck " (*Ægialitis Wilsonius,*
Cass.).   Said to occur ; I have yet to meet with it.

172. **Squatarola helvetica**, Cuvier. — *Black-bellied
Plover,* " Beetle-head," " Bull-head."   Generally abundant
during the migrations, but sometimes not even common.

HÆMATOPODIDÆ, — Oyster-Catchers.

173. **Hæmatopus palliatus**, Temm. — *Oyster-Caicher.*
Accidental ; but one or two instances of its capture on
record.

174. **Strepsilas interpres**, Illig. — *Turnstone,* "Chick-
en Bird," " Red-legged Plover," " Black-heart," " Brant-
Bird."   Rather common on the coast during the migrations.
Frequents rocky shores.

SCOLOPACIDÆ, — The Snipes.

175. **Philohela minor**, Linn. — *Woodcock.*   Common
summer resident.   Arrives early in April.   Breeds, nesting
on the ground

176. **Gallinago Wilsonii**, Bon. — *Snipe,* " English
Snipe."   Common during the migrations.   Arrives early
in April , by November 30th they have all passed Massa·
chusetts on their southern migrations.

177. **Macrorhamphus griseus**, Leach.— *Red-breasted
Snipe,* " Robin Snipe," " Brown-back," " Dowitcher."   Not
uncommon during the migrations.

178. **Calidris arenaria,** Illig. — *Sanderling,* "Shore-Bird," " Beach-Bird." Abundant on the sandy shores and beaches during the migrations.

179. **Tringa canutus,** Linn. — *Knot,* "Gray-back." Common spring and autumn migrant.

180. **Arquatella maritima,** Baird. — *Purple Sand-piper,* "Rock Snipe." Never very common. Found on the coast during spring and autumn.

181. **Ancylocheilus subarquatus,** Kaup. — *Curlew Sandpiper.* — Accidental, or very rare. A few specimens taken on our coast.

182. **Pelidna Americana,** Coues. — *American Dunlin,* " Red-back." Abundant spring and autumn migrant. Have taken it late in November. I do not think it winters.

On June 18, 1868, I saw and shot several specimens of this Sandpiper about the fresh-water ponds on Ipswich beach ; they were fat, and, upon dissecting, the females did not exhibit any signs of breeding ; they were evidently the young of the preceding year.

183. **Actodromas maculata,** Cass. — *Pectoral Sand-piper,* "Jacksnipe," "Grass Bird," " Fat-Bird." Common during the migrations. Frequents the marshes.

184. **Actodromas minutilla,** Coues. — *Least Sand-piper,* " Peep." Abundant during the migrations.

185. **Actodromas Bonapartii,** Cass. — *Bonaparte's Sandpiper,* "White-rumped Sandpiper," "Grass-Bird." Abundant during the migrations. Frequents the marshes.

186. **Ereunetes pusillus,** Cass. — *Semipalmated Sand-piper,* "Peep." Abundant during the migrations. June 18, 1868, they were found in company with *P. Americana,* at Ipswich, and were in the same condition.

187. **Micropalama himantopus,** Baird. — *Stilt Sandpiper.* Very rare. A single specimen captured in autumn by Mr. W. Brewster, at Rye Beach, New Hampshire.*

* Mr. Brewster informs me that he took another at the same place in the last week in August, 1869.

188. **Symphemia semipalmata**, HARTL. — *Willet*, "Stone Curlew," "Humility." Rather rare summer resident. Frequents sandy shores. Has a loud note of alarm, which startles every bird on the shore within hearing. I have seen large numbers of this species perched on dead mangrove-trees in Florida.

189. **Gambetta melanoleuca**, BON. — *Telltale*, "Stone Snipe," "Winter Yellow-Legs," "Greater Tatler." Common during the migrations. Arrives from the north early in August.

190. **Gambetta flavipes**, BON. — *Yellow-Legs*, "Summer Yellow-Legs," "Lesser Tatler." Summer resident; common during the migrations. I have seen it at Ipswich on the marshes throughout the summer. Perhaps breeds.

191. **Rhyacophilus solitarius**, BAIRD. — *Solitary Sandpiper*, "Steelyard Bird." Not very common during the migrations. Remains late in the autumn. On October 31, 1869, when the ponds were partly frozen over, I shot a specimen in Errol, New Hampshire; it was much emaciated, but apparently well and lively. Although the birds have been seen in summer, yet no case of their actually breeding is recorded; probably this is a case parallel with those quoted above (*P. Americana* and *E. pusillus*).

192. **Tringoides macularius**, BON. — *Spotted Sandpiper*, "Tip-up," "Teter-tail." Common summer resident both on the shore and in the interior. Arrives from May 1st to 8th; leaves in September. Breeds, nesting, in the interior, on the edge of a rye-field, or near ploughed land; on the coast, in the sand or among the rocks.

193. **Actiturus Bartramius**, BON. — *Bartram's Sandpiper*, "Field Plover," "Hill-Bird," "Upland Plover," "Gray Plover." Not an uncommon summer resident; quite common during the migrations. Frequents the dry fields, where it breeds. Arrives about the last of April.

194. **Tryngites rufescens**, Cab.—*Buff-breasted Sand-piper*, "Little Plover." Rare spring and autumn migrant; found on the sandy shores.

195. **Limosa fedoa**, Ord. — *Marbled Godwit*, "Brant-Bird," "Badger-Bird." Rare during the migrations. Mr. H. B. Farley informs me that he shot a specimen at Ipswich on July 17, 1869. Winters in large numbers in Florida, and I was assured, upon good authority, that it remained during the summer, but the nest has never been found! How they propagated was a mystery to those unacquainted with its northern migration.

196. **Limosa Huds:nica**, Swain. — *Hudsonian Godwit*, "Goose-Bird," "Black-tail," "Spot-neck." Very rare during the migrations.

197. **Numenius longirostris**, Wils. — *Long-billed Curlew*, "Sickle-bill." Not uncommon during the migrations, but very shy; but few shot on this account.

198. **Numenius Huds:nicus**, Lath. — *Hudsonian Curlew*, "Dough-Bird," "Jack Curlew." Very rare on the migrations.

199. **Numenius borealis**, Lath. — *Esquimaux Curlew*, "Flute." Not uncommon during the migrations. The "Dough-Bird" of gunners. Very fat in autumn.

PHALAROPODIDÆ, — The Phalaropes.

200. **Steganopus Wilsonii**, Coues. — *Wilson's Phalarope*. Accidental on the coast. Audubon appears to be the only one who records it from this section.

201. **Phalaropus fulicarius**, Bon. — *Red Phalarope*. Occasional during the migrations along the coast.

202. **Lobipes hyperboreus**, Cuv. — *Northern Phalarope*. Not common during the migrations.

While migrating, the Phalaropes generally keep off the coast.

RECURVIROSTRIDÆ, — The Avosets and Stilts.

The American Avoset (*Recurvirostra Americana*, Gm.) may perhaps occur; no well-authenticated instance of its capture in the State is on record.

203. **Himantopus nigricollis**, Vieill. —*Black-necked Stilt*, "Lawyer." Occasionally seen along the sandy beaches.

Of this fact I am assured by gunners and others, who have noticed it on account of its peculiarities, and ironically named it "Humility."

ARDEIDÆ, — The Herons.

204. **Ardea herodias**, Linn. — *Great Blue Heron*, "Crane." Common summer resident. Probably breeds.

205. **Herodias egretta**, Gray. — *Great White Egret*. Accidental. Two specimens in the Museum of Comparative Zoölogy, taken at or near Hudson, by Mr. S. Jillson, in the autumn of 1867; one or two other instances on record of its capture in this section.

A magnificent mature specimen is in the fine collection of Mr. N. Vickery, which was shot at Lynn, near the railroad station.

206. **Garzetta candidissima**, Bon. — *Snowy Heron*, or *Little White Egret*. Entirely accidental. "Have seen one that was killed near Boston in 1862."* One other instance of its capture is on record. This and the preceding are stragglers from the south.

207. **Florida cærulea**, Baird. — *Little Blue Heron*. Rare summer visitor. I have met with it but twice in this section. A few other instances of its capture are on record.

* J. A. Allen, "Proceedings of the Essex Institute." IV 1864 p 86

208. **Ardetta exilis**, GRAY. — *Least Bittern*. Very rare in summer. Mr. William Brewster has a specimen in his cabinet, taken on the Fresh Pond marshes in Belmont, August 11, 1868.

209. **Botaurus lentiginosus**, STEPH. — *Bittern*, "Meadow Hen," "Indian Hen," "Dunkadoo." Common summer resident. Breeds, nesting in inaccessible places in swamps and fresh marshes. Arrives early in April; leaves in October. This species is rare on the sea-shore.

210. **Butorides virescens**, BON. — "Green Heron," "Mud-Hen," "Poke," "Chalk-line." Common summer resident. Breeds, nesting in thickets and thick woods, but more commonly on the sea-shore than in the interior.

211. **Nyctiardea Gardenii**, BAIRD. — *Night Heron*, "Qua-Bird," "Squak," "Gooly-gossit." Common summer resident, breeding abundantly in communities, both on the coast and in the interior. The young, when able to fly, congregate on the sea-shore. Although nocturnal in habit, it sees well by day. Arrives early in April; leaves in October.

As substantiating the hypothesis concerning the luminousness of the peculiar spot on the breast of this Heron, I give the following, as related to me by Mrs. H. B. Farley, of Ipswich. I may state that Mrs. Farley, until after she had related the story, had no knowledge of any particular interest being attached to the fact she had discovered; for this reason she was an unbiased observer, which gives the discovery additional importance.

" Three or four years ago I was sitting on the banks of Ipswich River, just at twilight, waiting for my brother to come for me in a boat to convey me home. I was keeping very quiet, when I saw a Heron alight within a few feet of me, on the edge of the water. He was joined by others, until there were about a dozen, then I observed that every one of them had a luminous spot on its breast. This spot was not very bright, but, as it was quite dark by this time, *plainly perceptible.* They presented a peculiar appearance as they walked about, and I watched them with interest for some time. This singular light surprised me much, as I had never heard of anything like it before."

It was in the autumn when Mrs. Farley observed this striking and interesting phenomenon.

212. **Nyctherodius violaceus**, REICH. — *Yellow-crowned Night Heron.* — Mr. Vickery informs me that he shot a specimen in Lynn in 1865. The bird was flying over his head at the time.

213. **Falcinellus Ordii**, BON. — *Glossy Ibis.* Accidental or occasional. Nuttall records one or two instances of its capture ; Cabot, one or two ; none recently, however. Mr. Vickery also informs me that he has seen a specimen of this fine bird, that was taken, fifteen years ago, at or near Stafford Ridge, New Hampshire.

RALLIDÆ, — THE RAILS.

214. **Rallus crepitans**, GM. — *Clapper Rail,* " Salt-marsh Hen." Accidental. Mr. J. F. Le Baron informed me that he shot a specimen, some years ago, at Ipswich. Also one taken by Mr. S. J. Cabot.

215. **Rallus Virginianus**, LINN. — *Virginia Rail.* Common summer resident. Frequents the bushy swamps. Breeds early, nesting on some tussock   Have seen the young running about by the first of June.

216. **Porzana Carolina**, VIEILL. — *Carolina Rail,* " Sora Rail," " Ortolan." Common summer resident. Frequents the wet, open meadows, where it breeds. Both of these species are much more common than most collectors or sportsmen are aware of. I have been in a swamp where

there were literally thousands of them, yet I was unable to start more than two or three! Indeed, without a good dog, trained for the purpose, it is impossible to secure any number. They leave early for the south.

217. **Porzana noveboracensis**, Cass. — *Yellow Rail.* Very rare during the migrations. Perhaps a few breed. On September 8, 1868, my young friend, Frank P. Jackson, was walking with me in the dusk of evening, through a squash-field, on *high land,* when he started up and shot a specimen. There was a meadow twenty or thirty rods away at the foot of the hill. It is a female, and differs from any I have ever seen, having *a broad white edging to the secondaries;* so broad and prominent is this edging, that it gave the bird the appearance of having white wings while flying, in the imperfect light in which it was shot.

218. **Fulica Americana**, Gm. — *Coot,* "Mud-Hen." Summer resident. Perhaps breeds. Generally seen during the migrations. Frequents the weedy edges of ponds and rivers.

219. **Gallinula galeata**, Bon. — *Common Gallinule, Florida Gallinule.* Accidental. A specimen taken on the Concord River marshes, in the fall of 1867, by Mr. T. Dewing. "The Florida Gallinule probably breeds in the Fresh Pond marshes, as I shot a young bird on October 9, 1868, and saw another." *

220. **Gallinula martinica**, Lath. — *Purple Gallinule.* Like the preceding. Accidental. A few specimens have been taken in the State.

ANATIDÆ, — The Swans, Geese, Ducks, etc.

221. **Cygnus Americanus**, Sharpless. — *Swan.* Very rare in winter, Mr. J. F. Le Baron informs me that in

* MS. Notes of Mr. W. Brewster.

former years this bird was occasionally seen at Ipswich ; but of late years it has not made its appearance.

The Snow Goose (*Anser hyperboreus*, Pallas) perhaps occurs rarely in winter.

The White-fronted Goose (*Anser Gambelii*, Hartl.), like the preceding, perhaps rarely occurs in the State.

The Barnacle Goose (*Bernicla leucopsis*). This European species has been attributed to this coast, but apparently upon insufficient evidence. It may, however, occur, as it has recently been detected and taken near the southern end of Hudson's Bay.*

222. **Bernicla brenta**, Steph. — *Brant.* Common spring and autumn migrant on the coast.

The Hutchin's Goose (*Bernicla Hutchinsii*, Bon.) perhaps occurs rarely during the migrations, as it has been taken in Connecticut.

223. **Bernicla canadensis**, Boie. — *Wild Goose.* Abundant spring and autumn migrant.

224. **Anas boschas**, Linn. — *Mallard.* Rare spring and autumn migrant.

225. **Anas obscura**, Gm. — *Black Duck.* Abundant winter resident. A few breed.

226. **Dafila acuta**, Jenyns. — *Pin-tail*, "Sprig-tail," "Pile-start." Rare winter resident along the coast.

227. **Nettion Carolinensis**, Baird. — *Green-winged Teal.* Common during the migrations.

228. **Nettion crecca**, Kaup. — *English Teal.* Straggling from Europe ; entirely accidental. "Has been taken in the State by Dr. H. Bryant."†

229. **Spatula clypeata**, Boie. — *Shoveller*, "Spoon-billed" Duck. Rare in spring and autumn.

230. **Querquedula discors**, Steph. — *Blue-winged Teal.* Common spring and autumn migrant.

---

* Professor S. F. Baird, in "American Naturalist," II. 1868, p. 49.

† J. A. Allen, "Proceedings of the Essex Institute," IV. 1864, p. 88.

231. **Chaulelasmus streperus,** GRAY. — *Gadwall,* "Gray Duck." Rare in spring and autumn.

232. **Mareca Penelope,** BON. — *European Widgeon.* Straggler from Europe. Mr. Samuels says it has been taken in the State.

233. **Mareca Americana,** STEPH. — *American Widgeon.* " Baldpate." Not uncommon during the migrations.

234. **Aix sponsa,** SWAIN. — *Wood Duck.* Common summer resident.

235. **Fulix marila,** BAIRD. — *Scaup Duck,* " Black-head, " Blue-bill." Not common on the migrations.

236. **Fulix affinis,** BAIRD. — *Little Black-head.* Rare during the migrations.

237. **Fulix collaris,** BAIRD. — *Ring-necked Duck.* Rare in spring and autumn. This and the three preceding frequent the ponds and rivers of the interior.

238. **Aythya Americana,** BON. — *Red-head.* Rare in autumn.

239. **Aythya vallisneria,** BON. — *Canvas-back.* Rare in autumn. Plentiful in Boston markets, but brought from farther south.

240. **Bucephala Americana,** BAIRD. — *Golden-Eye,* " Whistler." Common during winter. Exceedingly shy.

241. **Bucephala albeola,** BAIRD. — *Buffle-head,* " Butter-ball," " Dipper." Not uncommon in autumn and winter.

242. **Histrionicus torquatus,** BON. — *Harlequin Duck,* " Lord." Very rare during winter.

243. **Harelda glacialis,** LEACH. — *Long-tailed Duck,* " Old Wife," " Old Squaw," " South Southerly." Abundant spring and autumn migrant ; some winter.

244. **Camptolæmus Labradorius,** GRAY. — *Labrador Duck.* Rare during winter.

245. **Melanetta velvetina,** BAIRD. — *Velvet Duck,* " White-winged Coot," " Butter-bill." Common during winter on the coast.

246. **Pelionetta perspicillata,** Kaup. — *Surf-Duck,* "Coot." Common during autumn and winter.

247. **Œdemia Americana,** Swain. — *Scoter,* "Graywinged Coot." Abundant during autumn; common in winter.*

248. **Somateria mollissima,** Leach. — *Eider-Duck.* Common during spring and autumn, also on the south shore in winter.

249. **Somateria spectabilis,** Leach. — *King Eider.* Rare in winter.

250. **Erismatura rubida,** Bon. — *Ruddy Duck,* "Looby," "Dumb-Bird." Common during the migration in spring and autumn. Seen on ponds in the interior.

251. **Mergus Americanus,** Cass. — *Sheldrake,* "Gooseander," "Fish Duck." Common during the migrations. Seen on ponds in the interior.

252. **Mergus serrator,** Linn. — *Red-breasted Merganser,* "Sheldrake," "Wheaser." Abundant during the migrations.

253. **Lophodytes cucullatus,** Reich. — *Hooded Merganser,* "Water-Pheasant." Not common during the migrations. Abundant in Florida in winter.

PELECANIDÆ, — The Pelicans.

254. **Pelecanus fuscus,** Linn.† — *Brown Pelican.* Mr. J. F. Le Baron is confident of having seen two of this species at Ipswich some years ago.

255. **Pelecanus erythrorhynchus,** Gm. — *White Pelican.* Mr. Allen informs me that a specimen was recently taken at Brant Point, Nantucket.

---

* Mr. E. C. Greenwood informs me that this, with the two preceding species, is sometimes seen in summer.

† Erroneously given by Mr Allen as the succeeding species, "American Naturalist," III. p. 640.

SULIDÆ, — The Gannets.

256. **Sula bassana,** Ross. — *Gannet,* "Haglett." Common in winter off the coast.

257. **Sula fiber,** Linn. — *Booby.* Given as rare in Essex County, some years ago, by Mr. Putnam ; no record of its capture recently.

GRACULIDÆ, — The Cormorants.

258. **Graculus dilophus,** Gray. — *Double-crested Cormorant,* "Shag." Not uncommon off the coast in winter.

259. **Graculus carbo,** Gray. — *Common Cormorant,* "Shag." Common off the coast in autumn and winter.

LARIDÆ, — The Gulls, Terns, etc.

260. **Buphagus Skua,** Coues. — *Skua Gull.* Said to be rare on the coast ; perhaps doubtful.

261. **Stercorarius pomarinus,** Temm. — *Pomarine Skua or Jäger.* Not uncommon along the coast in autumn and winter.

262. **Stercorarius parasiticus,** Gray. — *Arctic Jäger.* Rare in winter off the coast.

263. **Stercorarius Buffonii,** Coues. — *Long-tailed Jäger,* "Marlinspike." Not uncommon off the coast in winter.

264. **Larus marinus,** Linn. — *Great Black-backed Gull,* "Saddle-back," "Coffin-carrier." Common during winter.

265. **Larus glaucus,** Brunn. — *Glaucous Gull,* "Ice Gull." Rare in winter.

266. **Larus leucopterus,** Faber. — *White-winged Gull.* Not common in winter.

267. **Larus argentatus**, BRUNN. — *Herring Gull.* Common resident ; more abundant in autumn and winter. Does not now breed anywhere in the State, although it did formerly; those remaining in summer are mostly immature birds.

268. **Larus Delawarensis**, ORD. — *Ring-billed Gull.* Not uncommon along the coast in winter.

The Hutchin's Gull (*Larus Hutchinsii*, Richardson). A specimen taken in Salem harbor, 1856, in the museum of the Peabody Academy of Science, labelled by Dr. Coues as above ; it, however, looks very like an albino ; perhaps *L. argentatus.*

269. **Chrœcocephalus atricilla**, LEACH. — *Laughing Gull.* Not uncommon along the whole coast. Have found it breeding at Muskegat Island, south of the main-land, and near Nantucket. I should judge that there were a dozen pairs breeding. Does not breed elsewhere on the coast. Have seen an egg and bird taken at Tenant's Harbor, Maine, by Mr. L. L. Thaxter, of Newton. I have seen the bird late in November at Ipswich.

270. **Chrœcocephalus Philadelphia**, LEACH. — *Bonaparte's Gull.* Common in autumn and spring, a few winter.

271. **Rissa tridactyla**, BON. — *Kittiwake.* Common in autumn and winter.

The Marsh Tern (*Gelochelidon Anglica*, Bon.) is said to occur ; if it does, I have yet to meet with it.

272. **Thalasseus Caspius**, BOI. — *Caspian Tern.* Rare in winter. I have seen it upon one or two occasions ; have also seen it in New York harbor in December.

273. **Thalasseus acuflavida**, CABOT. — *Cabot's Tern, Sandwich Tern.* Mr. Vickery has a fine specimen of this bird in his cabinet, that he took at Cape Cod in the autumn of 1866. He also saw another. This specimen is

in immature plumage. Its usual habitat is from Texas to Florida and the West Indies.

274. **Sterna hirundo**, LINN. — *Wilson's Tern.* Abundant on the coast in summer. Breeds abundantly on the sandy beaches and islands. This species, and also *S. macroura*, are called, by popular writers, " Seamews." They are also called " Tide Gulls " and " Meous."

275. **Sterna macroura**, NAUM. — *Arctic Tern.* Abundant summer resident. I do not think it winters. Breeds abundantly along the shore. Found it at Muskegat, breeding apart from the other species. There is no difference in the note between this and *S. hirundo.*

The descriptions heretofore given of this bird have been meagre, and in many cases erroneous, tending to produce doubt as to its validity as a species. But as the specific characters are well defined, and certain of them so constant as fully to establish its claim as a species, I purpose to give here a full description of it, with a table of measurements.

Sterna macroura, NAUM. — *Arctic Tern, Red-billed Tern.*

Sterna macroura.	NAUM., Isis 1819, 1847.
" *macrura.*	LAWR., Birds N Am. 1858, p. 862.
" *macroura*	COUES, Proceedings Phil. Acad. N. S., Dec., 1862, p. 549.
Sterna arctea	" TEMM , Mar. d'Orn., II., 1820, p. 742."
" "	BON., Syn. 1828, No 287, p. 354.
" "	SW. & RICH., F B A., II., 1831, p. 414.
" "	NUTT., Man . II , 1834, p 275.
" "	AUD., Orn. Biog , III., 1835, p. 296. — IB. Birds Am. VII. 1844. p 107; Pl. CCCCXXIV.*
" "	Dr H. Bryant, Pro Boston Soc. of Nat. Hist. VI., 1858, p. 120.

SP. CH. — *Adult.* Bill slender, slightly curved ; color, bright carmine. Top of head and hind neck, black. Neck, back, wing-coverts, scapularies, secondaries, breast, and

* Figures *S. hirundo* with black tip to bill.

sides, a beautiful pearl gray, except the inner edge of the secondaries, with their tips, and those of the scapularies, which are white. Quills, with the upper parts gray, dusky towards the tips, with the outer web of the outer feather, and a narrow basal line along the inner web of the terminal portion of each feather, black. Basal portion and shaft of each feather, together with the margins of the inner webs and whole under surface of the wing, white. Rump, upper tail-coverts, tail-feathers, abdomen, and under tail-coverts, pure white, except the terminal portion of the outer webs of the two outer tail-feathers on each side, which are dusky. The chin, upper part of the throat, and a line running from the base of the bill under the eye to the occiput, also white; the chin and throat are sometimes tinged with ashy. The under eyelids are black. Feet, small; tarsus, short. The transverse scales on the tarsi and toes are very much ridged; the upper part of the webs and under surface of the feet are covered with small, granulous protuberances; both of these facts give the feet a peculiar appearance. Color, bright vermilion.

Young. — The young-of-the-year, the ensuing spring, differs from this in having the bill *longer, thicker, and more curved*, with a small part of the basal and a spot near the tip of the upper mandible dusky; the bill is not so intense in color. There are a few white feathers near the base of the bill in the black of the head. The upper parts generally, with the exceptions of the wing-coverts, which are *darker*, are lighter. The outer webs of all the tail-feathers are dusky. The under parts are paler. The feet are not so intense in color.

*Young-of-the-year in autumn** differs from the preceding

---

* This stage of plumage has been before unknown to authors, at which I am somewhat surprised. The specimens that I am describing were shot with the old, who exhibited considerable solicitude.

7 *

Measurements of S. macroura.

No.	Locality.	Age.	Sex.	Length.	Stretch.	Wing.	Tail.	Bill along Culmen.	Bill from Gape.	Bill along Gonys.	Leg.	Tarsus.	Date.	Remarks.
863	Ipswich	Adult	♀	15.00	30.75	10.60	6.49	1.27	1.82	—	4.30	.56	July 1, 1868	Breeding.
829	Muskegat	"	♀	14.75	30.25	10.70	6.90	1.20	2.00	.80	2.80	.60	"	"
951	"	"	♂	15.50	30.50	10.75	7.45	1.28	2.08	.88	2.90	.68	"	"
952	"	"	—	16.60	30.95	11.20	8.25	1.35	1.90	.88	2.85	.71	"	"
953	"	"	♀	14.10	29.30	10.12	6.25	1.25	1.90	.84	2.90	.69	"	"
954	"	"	♂	14.50	31.00	10.00	6.80	1.25	—	—	2.90	.66	"	"
956	"	"	♂	15.00	21.00	11.84	8.30	1.25	—	—	2.76	.65	July 2, 1868	"
966	"	"	♂	15.00	32.28	11.50	7.60	1.30	—	—	2.96	.61	"	"
960	"	"	♀	15.15	29.75	11.00	7.74	1.20	—	—	2.80	.60	"	"

No.	Locality	Age	Sex										Date	Breeding
961	Muskegat	Adult	♂	15.75	31.20	11.25	6.50	1.32	—	—	3.10	.65	July 2, 1868	Breeding.
932	"	"	♂	15.15	32.15	11.50	7.50	1.33	—	—	2.70	.65	"	"
933	"	"	♂	13.00	32.75	11.75	6.00	1.30	—	—	3.00	.61	"	"
990	"	"	♂	14.70	29.40	11.08	6.75	1.35	—	—	2.86	.60	"	"
991	"	"	♂	15.75	30.50	11.00	7.30	1.35	—	—	3.07	.65	"	"
992	"	"	♂	14.50	29.00	10.70	4.30	1.28	—	—	2.75	.65	"	"
993	"	"	♀	15.00	31.25	11.00	7.85	1.35	—	—	2.95	.62	"	"
994	"	"	♂	15.40	30.50	11.50	6.00	1.32	—	—	3.00	.62	"	"
893	"	"	♂	17.00	31.25	11.70	7.51	1.26	—	—	2.60	.60	"	"
897	"	2 years	♂	16.75	31.50	10.80	7.26	1.35	—	—	2.85	.52	"	"
2045	Ipswich	Adult	♂	16.00	31.50	11.00	7.75	1.40	1.90	.95	—	.60	July 31, 1869	With young.
2044	"	"	♂	16.00	31.00	11.75	7.75	1.30	1.95	.80	—	.60	"	"
2042	"	Young fledgling	♂	15.25	31.00	11.50	7.50	1.25	1.90	.75	—	.56	"	Just able to fly.
2050	"	Adult	♂	17.25	30.75	11.75	7.25	1.25	1.95	—	—	.65	"	With young.
2919	"	"	♂	15.50	30.75	—	7.90	1.25	1.75	—	—	.65	"	"
2946	"	Young-of-year	♂	8.75	20.15	7.50	1.90	1.16	—	—	—	.60	"	Flew well.
2939	"	"	♀	11.50	23.75	8.00	2.60	.85	1.10	.51	—	.67	"	Very young.

in having the forehead quite white; a few white feathers on the back of the head; the black is not quite as intense, or more brownish. The feathers of the back are edged with rufous. The shoulders are darker. The tail is not as deeply forked, and the tips of the feathers are rufous. The whole under parts are pure white. The white line from the base of the bill is discontinued just in front of the eye, and the portion occupied by it is quite *dusky, almost black!* The feet are dull orange. The bill is black, with the base of the lower mandible orange.

The *S. hirundo* differs from this species, in the adult stage, in having the beak longer and more curved, with the color bright orange, and the terminal portion *always* black. The pearl gray of the upper and under parts is never as deep, while the lower part of the back is always quite pale, so that the white of the rump is not as abrupt in its commencement. The throat and chin are *always* white, without the ashy tinge. The feet are larger, the tarsi much longer. The tarsi also lack the ridged transverse scales; they are smoother; the webs are also smooth; the color is pale orange, never approaching the carmine of the other.

In the next stage there is more white on the head of *S. hirundo;* the bill is almost black; the rump tinged with ashy.

Young-of-the-year birds are readily distinguished by the rump of *hirundo* being ashy, the feet larger, the tarsi longer with a smoother appearance. The bill is much the same color, but in *hirundo* it is longer. It never has the dusky appearance below the eye seen in *macroura.*

276. **Sterna paradisea** — *Roseate Tern.* This, with the two preceding species, is called the "Mackerel Gull" on the more northern sections of the coast, while on the south shore the two preceding are called "Té-arrs," from the note; this species is called "Hoyt" for the same reason.

Common at Ipswich in autumn. Abundant on the south shore during the breeding-season. Breeds on Muskegat Island abundantly ; generally building a nest of sticks in a hollow among the Sand-hills.

277. **Sterna Antillarum**, Coues. — *Least Tern,* "Jack-knife Gull." Not as common as the preceding. Breeds later, not until July ; lays from one to four eggs. Have found a few breeding at Ipswich. Also breeds on Nantucket.

Forster's Tern (*Sterna Forsterii*, Nutt). This species appears to differ from *hirundo* in having the outer web of the outer tail-feather *white.* I have never met with it.

278. **Hydrochelidon fissipes**, Gray. — *Short-tailed Tern.* Rare in autumn. Mr. J. F. Le Baron shot a specimen at Ipswich, August 11, and saw another.

279. **Haliplana fuliginosa**, Wagl. — *Sooty Tern.* Mr. Samuels says he "found it breeding on Muskegat Island." I think it occurs rarely.

PROCELLARIDÆ, — The Petrels.

280. **Puffinus major**, Faber. — *Greater Shearwater.* Not uncommon off the coast in winter.

281. **Puffinus Anglorum**, Temm. — *Mank's Shearwater.* Rare off the coast in winter.

282. **Puffinus fuliginosus**, Strickl. — *Sooty Shearwater.* Common off the coast during spring, autumn, and winter.

283. **Procellaria pelagica**, Linn. — *Stormy Petrel.* Rare off the coast.

284. **Oceanites oceanica**, Coues. — *Wilson's Petrel.* Common off the coast.

285. **Cymochorea leucorrhoa**, Coues. — *Leach's Petrel.* Abundant off the coast. This and the two pre-

ceding are the "Mother Carey's Chickens" of sailors and
others. On September 9, 1869, after a gale, a specimen
was shot on Charles River, twelve miles from the sea!

COLYMBIDÆ, — The Divers and Loons.

286. Colymbus torquatus, Brunn. — *Great North
ern Diver*, "Loon." Common in autumn, winter, and spring.
Breeds in western Massachusetts; I do not think it does
in this section.

287. Colymbus arcticus, Linn. — *Black-throated
Loon*, or *Diver*. Very rare during winter.

288. Colymbus septentrionalis, Linn. — *Red-
throated Loon*, or *Diver*. The most common of all the
species during the winter and autumn, called everywhere
"Cape Race," or "Scapegrace," by gunners.

PODICIPIDÆ, — The Grebes.

289. Podiceps Holböllii, Reinhardt. — *Red-necked
Grebe*, "Dipper Duck." Common during the migrations.

290. Podiceps cristatus, Lath. — *Crested Grebe*.
Common during autumn and winter.

291. Podiceps cornutus, Lath.—*Horned Grebe*. Common during autumn and winter. This and the two preceding frequent the salt water exclusively. Are seldom
met with in full plumage. Called by gunners "Devil
Divers" and "Water Witches," on account of their diving
to elude the shot; their power of diving and remaining
under water a long time is certainly marvellous.

292. Podilymbus podiceps, Lawr. — *Dabchick*.
"Dipper Duck." Common during the migrations. fre
quents the fresh waters.

ALCIDÆ, — The Auks and Guillemots.

The Great Auk (*Alca impennis*, Linn.) must have been quite common many years ago on the coast north of Cape Ann. In the autumn of 1867, and in company with Mr. Allen in June, 1868, I found in the shell-heaps on the Ipswich Sand-hills, numerous bones of this now extinct bird; probably dropped there by the Indians,* who must have killed them with their arrows, or other primitive weapons, for food.

293. **Utamania torda,** Leach. — *Razor-billed Auk,* "Tinker." Common in winter off the coast.

294. **Fratercula arctica,** Illig. — *Puffin,* "Sea Par rot." Not uncommon in winter off the coast.

295. **Uria grylle,** Lath. — *Black Guillemot,* "Sea Pigeon." Common in winter.

296. **Lomvia troille,** Brandt. — *Foolish Guillemot,* "Murre." Common off the coast in winter.

297. **Lcmvia ringvia,** Brandt. — *Murre.* Not uncommon in winter off the coast.

298. **Lcmvia Svarbag,** Coues. — *Brünnich's Guillemot, Thick-billed Guillemot.* Common off the coast in winter.

299. **Mergulus alle,** Vieill. — *Sea Dove,* "Doveke," "Little Auk." Common winter resident. I have seen it on Indian River, Florida.

* See account of Ipswich Sand-hills, pp. 54, 55

APPENDIX.

THE whole number of birds belonging to the fauna of
eastern Massachusetts is two hundred and ninety-nine,[*]
as will be seen by the Catalogue. Of these twelve have
been recently added, viz. : the Varied Thrush (*Turdus
nævius*), the Tennessee Warbler (*Helminthophaga peregrina*), the Baird's Sparrow (*Centronyx Bairdii*), the Gray
King-Bird (*Tyrannus Dominicensis*), the Yellow-headed
Blackbird (*Xanthocephalus icterocephalus*), the Barn Owl
(*Strix pratincola*), the Hawk Owl (*Surnia ulula*), the Stilt
Sandpiper (*Micropalama himantopus*), the Yellow-crowned
Night Heron (*Nyctherodius violaceus*), the Sandwich Tern
(*Sterna cantiaca*), the White Pelican (*Pelecanus erythro-
rhynchus*), and the Brown Pelican (*Pelecanus fuscus*).

In the following tables may be found a classification of

[*] The whole number of species given by Mr. J. A. Allen, in the "Proceedings of the Essex Institute," Vol. IV. No. 2, August, 1864, as occurring
in the State, was two hundred and ninety-six. Of these, three have not
been found in eastern Massachusetts, viz. : *Helminthophaga celata*, *Empidonax Acadicus*, and *Centurus Carolinus*. Those given upon doubtful or
insufficient evidence as birds of eastern Massachusetts, which are not included in the present list, are nine, viz.: *Parus Hudsonicus*, *Cardinalis
Virginianus*, *Ægialitis Wilsonius*, *Anser hyperboreus*, *Anser Gambelii*, *Bernicla Hutchinsii*, *Bernicla leucopsis*, *Procellaria glacialis*, and *Sterna ara-
nea*. Sixteen species are added in Mr. Allen's supplement (" American
Naturalist," Vol. III., pp. 505–519, 568–585, 631–648, 1869), after ex-
punging four species from the previous list, — increasing his catalogue to
three hundred and eight. Out of these, three are birds of western Massachusetts, viz.: *Nauclerus furcatus*, *Seiurus Ludovicianus*, and *Serinus meri-
dionalis*. Two of those given in his supplement as birds of eastern Massachusetts are not included in the present Catalogue, viz : *Buteo Cooperi* (not
included, for reasons given on page 135) and *Carduelis elegans*, which,
as Mr. Allen justly remarks, was probably an escaped cage-bird.

K

the birds of eastern Massachusetts, relative to their being resident, migratory, or straggling species, etc. : —

RESIDENT SPECIES THAT BREED.

1. Ampelis cedrorum.
2. Anas obscura. *
3. Astragalinus tristis. †
4. Astur atricapillus.
5. Bonasa umbellus.
6. Brachyotus Cassinii.
7. Bubo Virginianus.
8. Buteo lineatus.
9. Buteo borealis.
10. Carpodacus purpureus. †
11. Certhia familiaris. *
12. Colaptes auratus. †
13. Corvus Americanus. †
14. Cupidonia cupido.
15. Cyanura cristata. †
16. Falco columbarius. ‡
17. Falco sparverius. ‡
18. Melospiza melodia. ‡
19. Nyctale Acadica.
20. Ortyx Virginiana.
21. Otus Wilsonianus.
22. Parus atricapillus. †
23. Picus pubescens.
24. Picus villosus. †
25. Passer domestica.
26. Scops asio.
27. Sturnella magna. ‡
28. Syrnium nebulosum.
29. Turdus migratorius. §

* The greater part go north in summer, and south in winter.

† Those marked in this manner are not resident individually: that is, those species that have passed the summer with us migrate to the south, and others, who have passed the summer farther north, take their places. See remarks on page 129 under the head of *Picus villosus*.

‡ Of these species but few remain in winter, the greater part pass south.

§ Sometimes not to be found *all* winter.

RESIDENT SPECIES THAT DO NOT BREED.

1. Cymochorea leucorrhoa.
2. Haliætus leucocephalus. *
3. Larus argentatus. †
4. Melanetta velvetina. ‡
5. Oceanites oceanica.
6. Œdemia Americana. ‡
7. Pelionetta perspicillata. ‡

* This eagle is quite frequently seen along our coast, even in summer, but as it is not known to breed, and being a bird of strong flight, it is probable that it is making daily excursions in search of food.

† Those that remain during the summer are generally immature birds, probably the young of the previous year. See remarks on page 151, under *Larus argentatus*.

‡ These three species are given upon the authority of Mr. E. C. Greenwood, of Ipswich.

REGULAR SUMMER VISITANTS THAT BREED.

1. Accipiter Cooperii.
2. Accipiter fuscus.
3. Actiturus Bartramius.
4. Ægialitis melodus.
5. Ægialitis vociferus.
6. Agelæus phœniceus.
7. Aix sponsa.
8. Ammodromus caudacutus.
9. Antrostomus vociferus.
10. Ardea herodias.
11. Botaurus lentiginosus.
12. Buteo Pennsylvanicus.
13. Butorides virescens.
14. Ceryle alcyon.
15. Chætura pelasgia.
16. Chordeiles popetue.
17. Chrœcocephalus atricilla.
18. Circus Hudsonius.
19. Cistothorus palustris.
20. Cistothorus stellaris.
21. Coccygus Americanus.
22. Coccygus erythrophthalmus.
23. Contopus borealis.
24. Contopus virens.
25. Coturniculus Henslowi.
26. Coturniculus passerinus.
27. Cotyle riparia.
28. Cyanospiza cyanea.
29. Dendrœca æstiva.
30. Dendrœca discolor.
31. Dendrœca Pennsylvanica.
32. Dendrœca pina.
33. Dendrœca virens.
34. Dolichonyx oryzivorus.
35. Empidonax minimus.
36. Geothlypis trichas.
37. Guiraca Ludoviciana.
38. Harporhynchus rufus.
39. Helminthophaga chrysoptera.
40. Helminthophaga ruficapilla.
41. Hirundo horreorum.
42. Icterus Baltimore.
43. Icterus spurius. *
44. Melospiza palustris.
45. Mimus Carolinensis.
46. Mniotilta varia.
47. Molothrus pecoris.
48. Myiarchus crinitus. *
49. Nyctiardea Gardenii.
50. Parula Americana.†
51. Passerculus savanna.
52. Petrochelidon lunifrons.
53. Philohela minor.
54. Pipilo erythrophthalmus.
55. Pocecetes gramineus.
56. Porzana Carolina.
57. Progne subis.
58. Pyranga rubra.
59. Quiscalus versicolor.
60. Rallus Virginianus.
61. Sayornis fuscus.
62. Seiurus aurocapillus.
63. Setophaga ruticilla.
64. Sialia sialis.
65. Sitta Canadensis.†
66. Sitta Carolinensis.
67. Spizella pusilla.
68. Spizella socialis.
69. Sterna Antilarum.
70. Sterna hirundo.
71. Sterna macroura.
72. Sterna paradisea.
73. Tachycineta bicolor.
74. Tringoides macularius.
75. Trochilus colubris.
76. Troglodytes aëdon.
77. Turdus fuscescens.
78. Turdus mustelinus.

79. Turdus Pallasii.†
80. Tyrannus Carolinensis.
81. Vireo flavifrons.
82. Vireo gilvus.

83. Vireo noveboracensis.
84. Vireo olivaceus.
85. Vireo solitarius.†
86. Zenædura Carolinensis.

* These species breed only in small numbers. Massachusetts is about their extreme northern limit.

† These breed sparsely; the greater part go north.

REGULAR SUMMER VISITORS THAT DO NOT BREED.*

1. Ereunetes pusillus.
2. Gambetta flavipes.

3. Pelidna Americana.

* But few remain; the greater part go north. See remarks upon page 140, under the head of the preceding names.

IRREGULAR SUMMER VISITORS OR STRAGGLERS THAT HAVE BEEN KNOWN ·TO BREED.

1. Euspiza Americana.

2. Gallinula galeata

IRREGULAR SUMMER VISITORS OR STRAGGLERS THAT NEVER HAVE BEEN KNOWN TO BREED.

1. Ardetta exilis.
2. Argyria maculata.
3. Cathartes atratus.
4. Cathartes aura.
5. Chondestes grammacus.
6. Falcinellus Ordii.
7. Florida cærulea.
8. Gallinula martinica.
9. Garzetta candidissima.
10. Halipana fulignosa.
11. Herodias egretta.
12. Himantopus nigricollis.
13. Icteria viridis.

14. Melanerpes erythrocephalus.
15. Micropalama himantopus.
16. Mimus polyglottus.
17. Nyctherodius violaceus.
18. Pelecanus fuscus.*
19. Pelecanus erythrorhynchus.*
20. Pyranga æstiva.
21. Rallus crepitans.
22. Symphemia semipalmata.
23. Strix pratincola.†
24. Thalasseus acuflavida.†
25. Tyrannus Dominicensis.
26. Xanthocephalus icterocephalus.*

* Generally immature specimens, commonly taken in early autumn.

† One specimen captured in autumn.

That so many of these stragglers have been recently added to the catalogue must be attributed to the increased numbers of observers, rather than to the increase of specimens. Numerous instances like the preceding have undoubtedly occurred in the past, but from the scarcity of observers they have passed unnoticed, or at least unrecorded.

REGULAR SPRING AND AUTUMN MIGRANTS.

1. Actodromus Bonapartii.
2. Actodromus maculata.
3. Actodromus minutella.
4. Ægialitis semipalmatus.
5. Ammodromus maritimus.
6. Anas boschas.
7. Anorthura hyemalis.
8. Anthus Ludovicianus.
9. Arquatella maritima.
10. Aythya Americana.
11. Aythya vallisneria.
12. Bernicla brenta.
13. Bernicla Canadensis.*
14. Calidris arenaria.
15. Charadrius Virginicus.
16. Dafila acuta.
17. Dendrœca Blackburniæ.†
18. Dendrœca castanea.
19. Dendrœca cœrulescens.
20. Dendrœca coronata.
21. Dendrœca maculosa.
22. Dendrœca palmarum.
23. Dendrœca striata.
24. Empidonax flaviventris.
25. Erismatura rubida.
26. Fulica Americana.
27. Fulix affinis.
28. Fulix collaris.
29. Fulix marila.
30. Gallinago Wilsonii.
31. Gambetta melanoleuca.
32. Geothlypis Philadelphia.
33. Harelda glacialis.
34. Helminthophaga peregrina.‡
35. Hydrochelidon fissipes.§
36. Limosa fedoa.
37. Limosa Hudsonica.
38. Lophodytes cucullatus.
39. Macrorhamphus griseus.
40. Mareca Americana.
41. Myiodioctes Canadensis.‖
42. Myiodioctes pusillus.
43. Nettion Carolinensis.
44. Numenius borealis.
45. Numenius Hudsonicus.
46. Numenius longirostris.
47. Oporornis agilis.§
48. Pandion Carolinensis.
49. Passerella iliaca.
50. Perissoglossa tigrina.
51. Podilymbus podiceps.
52. Querquedula discors.
53. Regulus calendulus.
54. Rhyacophilus solitarius.
55. Scolecophagus ferrugineus.
56. Seiurus noveboracensis.†
57. Sphyrapicus varius.
58. Squatarola helvetica.
59. Strepsilas interpres.
60. Tringa canutus.

61. Troglodytes hyemalis.
62. Tryngites rufescens.
63. Turdus Swainsonii.
64. Zonotrichia leucophrys.
65. Zonotrichia albicollis.

* Probably breeds occasionally, as it certainly did in former years.
† Stragglers may remain and breed.
‡ Seen only in spring.
§ More common in autumn.
‖ Has been known to breed in the State.

OCCASIONAL OR IRREGULAR SPRING AND AUTUMN MIGRANTS.

1. Ancylocheilus subarquatus.
2. Chaulelasmus streperus.
3. Empidonax Traillii.
4. Hæmatopus palliatus.
5. Helminthophaga pina.
6. Lobipes hyperboreus. *
7. Mareca Penelope.†
8. Melospiza Lincolnii.
9. Nettion crecca.†
10. Phalaropus fulicarius. *
11. Porzana noveboracensis.
12. Procellaria pelagica. *
13. Spatula clypeata.
14. Steganopus Wilsonii. *

* These probably pass outside regularly, but seldom alight upon the shore.
† Accidental in autumn.

REGULAR WINTER VISITANTS.

1. Archibuteo logopus.
2. Archibuteo Sancti-Johannis.
3. Bucephala albeola. *
4. Bucephala Americana.
5. Camptolæmus Labradorius.
6. Chrœcocephalus Philadelphia.
7. Collurio borealis.
8. Colymbus septentrionalis.
9. Colymbus torquatus. *
10. Ectopistes migratorius.†
11. Eremophila alpestus.
12. Fratercula arctica.
13. Graculus carbo.‡
14. Graculus dilophus.‡
15. Histrionicus torquatus.
16. Junco hyemalis. *
17. Larus Delawarensis.
18. Larus glaucus.
19. Larus marinus.
20. Larus leucopterus.
21. Lomvia ringvia.
22. Lomvia Svarbag.
23. Lomvia troille.
24. Mergulus alle.
25. Mergus Americana.
26. Mergus serrator.
27. Nyctea nivea.
28. Plectrophanes Lapponicus.
29. Plectrophanes nivalis.
30. Podiceps cornutus.
31. Podiceps cristatus.
32. Podiceps Holbollii.
33. Puffinus Anglorum.‡
34. Puffinus fuliginosus.‡

35. Pulfinus major.‡
36. Regulus satrapus.
37. Rissa tridactyla.
38. Somateria mollissima.
39. Spizella monticola. *
40. Stercorarius Buffonii.

41. Stercorarius pomarinus.
42. Sula bassana.
43. Thalasseus Caspius.
44. Uria grylle.
45. Utamania torda.

* A few winter, but the greater part pass south.
† Generally seen in autumn, but a few winter.
‡ Seldom seen on the shore, but common off the coast.

WINTER VISITORS WHOSE OCCURRENCE MAY BE EXPECTED AT IRREGULAR PERIODS.

1. Ægiothus linarius.
2. Chrysomitris pinus.
3. Curvirostra Americana.

4. Curvirostra leucoptera.
5. Pinicola Canadensis.

IRREGULAR AND STRAGGLING WINTER VISITORS.

1. Ampelis garrulus. *
2. Aquila Canadensis.
3. Buphagus skua.
4. Centronyx Bairdii.†
5. Colymbus arcticus.
6. Cygnus Americanus.
7. Falco anatum.
8. Falco sacer.
9. Nyctale Richardsonii.

10. Picoides arcticus.
11. Picoides hirsutus.
12. Somateria spectabilis.
13. Stercorarius parasiticus.
14. Sula fiba.
15. Surnia ulula.
16. Syrnium cinereum.
17. Tetrao Canadensis.
18. Turdus nævius.†

* Occasionally seen in autumn.
† But one specimen taken.

INDEX TO PART II.

THE END.

www.ingramcontent.com/pod-product-compliance
Lightning Source LLC
Chambersburg PA
CBHW020537270326
41927CB00006B/616